MUSLIM BROTHERS IN LOCK-UP, U.S.A.

By

Faheem Majeed

TABLE OF CONTENTS

INTRODUCTION

Once upon a time the events in this work occurred, but as time moves, so do change.

All praise is due to Allah for sending the last Prophet and Messenger to the world, who was revealed the Holy Quran over 1418 years ago, the Prophet Muhammad, peace and blessings be upon him (pbuh). I bear witness that there is no Lord but Allah and that Prophet Muhammad (pbuh) is his last Messenger.

The direction that Al-Islam provides to a person while they are cut off from what's referred to as the free society, as in this case, the penitentiary, and then if that person enters into the ranks of an Islamic community to be used as an umbrella to grow under, the power of transformation begins to take place.

Those who strive to redeem themselves from the shackles of the self-defeating behaviors that landed them in the penitentiaries of North America know how the power of Al-Islam can transform those negative behaviors into something productive in their lives.

The focus of this work will be on those individuals who are making a conscientious effort to turn their lives around while still striving to implement the teachings of Al-Islam in their lives, while serving time in the penitentiaries of North America.

Those men and women, who at one point in their lives had to experience the test of coming to the penitentiary, in conjunction with the other trials that Allah said in the Holy Quran, that he would bring upon them, found that when some of the excess baggage has been stripped away, and they became isolated form those harmful influences, they were able to see the flawed character traits more clearer and then eradicate them from their behavior.

The Holy Quran, in chapter forty-seven, verse thirty-one, in the Abdullah Yusef Ali edition, Allah says, "And we shall try you, until we test those among you who strive their utmost, and persevere in patience and we shall try your reported mettle."

Al-Islam has been studied by social scientists and others, not only to see the effects that the teachings have on what's called the free society, but also on those in the penitentiary. What type of teachings can transform those that were considered incorrigible by the established societies standards, then turn around and become holders of degrees in Computer Science, Accounting, Psychology, Sociology, and Business; once they get the proper knowledge of self; with the most powerful vehicle for change being, Al-Islam.

In an environment where there's no privacy ninety-five percent of the time, and the privacy that one does have, is the thoughts that exist in one's own mind; perception plays a big part on how one person will react to another. A persons behavior is watched at all times and being that the emphasis is on order and discipline which calls for well-defined limits on what one may do, the repetitive acts of worship that the Muslims perform have an impact on everyone in the vicinity. Those that strive to put the principles of Al-Islam into practice throughout their stay in the penitentiary usually became examples for those around them.

Anytime a person claims to have a moral code, they'll be watched more closely than anyone else, with skepticism, mainly because of the constant bombardment of negativity that surrounds them on a daily basis, and therefore creates an idea of doubt within the observers minds, until they see consistency.

When an inmate decided to change his behavior and come into the religion of Al-Islam, the outward behavior is what other inmates' first notice. Inmates see brothers starting to perform their prayers five times a day and begin to ask, "You didn't do that on the streets, so why start now?" As Muslims, we know that Allah's mercy is always open to anyone who turns to him with sincere repentance, so when Muslims heard statements like that, there became an opportunity to engage in some dialogue concerning the religion of Al-Islam.

With no women or children around all day to interact with as part of a brother's family, the community of Muslim brothers becomes the family; for the five, ten, fifteen years or more that they do their time together.

With the time that brothers must do, there becomes a conscientious effort to establish an Islamic community, so that the knowledge that is studied can be implemented, at that point and not just when it's time to leave the penitentiary.

Because of the environment and oftentimes the repressive conditions that can be found in some penitentiaries, such as overzealous guards confronting brothers on a daily basis, overcrowding, and devious racist inmates; the books and instructions on war that can be found in the Holy Quran and the sayings and doings of the Prophet Muhammad (pbuh), becomes enticing. When brothers see barbed wire on top of and below the high fences that surround them, towers with guards in them with their weapons, and cameras located in strategic locations throughout the penitentiary, it becomes no mystery that a brother feels as though he's in a state of war. If it wasn't for the guidance of the Holy

Quran and sound sayings of the Prophet Muhammad (pbuh), to mode and tame the thirst

for liberation, once the teachings of Al-Islam is introduced to them, there would be

aggression out of control and blood spilt without just cause.

When inmates know that another inmate has become a Muslim, they'll watch to see

if the brother is performing his prayers. Because of the closeness that inmates have to be

towards one another over a number of years, inmates can't help but to notice one

another's habits. So with the Muslims being so entrenched for decades within the prisons

of America, inmates begin to expect a certain type of behavior from them, and if that

behavior is not in accord with what they've been seeing, they'll usually say so. "Ah, you

ain't doin' it like the other brothers, how come you don't get up in the morning to pray like

they do?"

No matter where brothers are at within the penitentiary, they will perform their

prayers at that moment. This is what helps the brothers to gain respect from the inmates

and prison authorities. In the dormitories, where there can be up to one hundred inmates

or more, depending on how overcrowded the system is, the brothers don't tell all the

inmates to shut up when it comes time to perform their prayers.

When a brother makes the call to prayer, the rest of the inmates will usually tone it

down, and if not, the brothers will ask them to hold it down. The majority of times that

method worked, but once in awhile the brothers had to speak the language of the people

that exist within the environment in which they live. This is the penitentiary, where some of

the hardest of the hard have been sent to, so adjustment by some inmates never comes

with just a polite request unless it's combined with some strength and power.

Sometimes in the gym, while basketball games are going on, or while there's some prison yard activities, brothers who may not have seen each other in a while, will perform their prayers together while other Muslims watch for them. Being on guard is an important aspect, because there is always vengeful acts being carried out by someone on the sneaky side; all the way from someone putting a contract on another inmate, to someone being crossed out of some money.

Unlike Islamic communities that can perform their prayers in their homes, temple or mosque, and not have to deal with contentious elements on a constant basis interfering with that privacy; there are no hideaways in an overcrowded environment, so therefore the right atmosphere has to be established, not by the guards, but by the Muslims themselves.

Establishing the right atmosphere without being offensive is the goal that brothers strive to accomplish. Many times when those who have gone through their life not being a part of anything meaningful, come into a disciplined way of life like Al-Islam, that begins to build some self-esteem; they get a rush, a feeling of elation. A sense of wanting to correct not only their own behavior, but also that which they perceive as unjust within their midst.

The atmosphere of the prison environment is what helps the Muslim brothers to determine how they're going to carry out their duties to Allah. In an environment where weakness is taken advantage of, there are still those inmates that see some Muslims bowing and then prostrating on the prayer rug, and then carrying themselves in a humble manner as a sign of weakness. In response to that type of thinking, brothers who were considered rough in the days before they came to the religion of, Al-Islam, became smoother in their roughness once they came into the religion, and therefore checked aggressive behavior.

One fact is known throughout the penal system in the United States, that the Muslim brothers are a group of people that don't go around looking for trouble. When confrontations do take place, every brother has been instructed to study the books of jihad (war) in order to at lest understand the positions that Muslims would take when confronted with conflict.

The Muslim brothers philosophy is one, that if they had to engage in skirmishes, small battles, and other little conflicts, it was going to be according to laws of the Holy Quran and sayings or doings of the Prophet Muhammad (pbuh), as close as possible.

The Muslim brothers that live, grow old, or die, doing their time striving to fulfill their obligations, finds satisfaction in the thought, that their deeds, bodily actions, and sacrifices of wealth are all due to Allah, the glorious and Most High.

With only the pilgrimage to Mecca, being the only pillar of the five that can't be fulfilled at the present time the walk to the Quranic and Islamic classes became the pilgrimage for them. So for those that will never get out of the penitentiary, this was considered the fulfillment of their obligation; Hajj (pilgrimage). In the prison society where the Muslims must live, the cellblocks and dormitories have other groups that have their own agendas. The gangs, who now refer to themselves as "organizations," racist groups who only raise their heads when they sense some weakness in other ethnic groups part and just regular inmates who are just doing their time by themselves. With that in mind, if something happens that affects the Muslim brothers (MB's), they don't call the police, guards, or anyone else to solve their problems for them, they take care of it themselves.

They police themselves, inside the world where there are different laws from those they were once in.

Security has to be developed; treaties have to be made between those different groups that have their own lifestyle, which may conflict with ones own, so that nothing gets out of hand. If something does get out of hand, preparations are made for war, to thwart those that move in an aggressive mode.

With all the interaction that goes on for years, it's incumbent for the (MB's) to strive to understand the Holy Quran, and the way that the Prophet Muhammad (pbuh) applied the laws of Al-Islam to his own situation in which he lived.

Studying the way Al-Islam had emerged, and under what circumstances the verses of the Holy Quran was revealed to the Prophet Muhammad (pbuh), provided the understanding that those verses weren't revealed in a vacuum. This told the brothers that it was vital for them to establish some sort of community life, no matter where they were at and not to do things on a whim, but with a purpose.

Of course, brothers would seek consultation with Emams on the streets when the circumstances warranted it. In a volatile environment, where things happened on the spur of the moment, within an enclosed setting, consultation would have to take place with those who were around you at the present time. A brother just couldn't get on the phone at any time of the day and say, "Assalaam Alaikum, brother, we need some advice concerning such and such."

The MB's use a chain of command that entails seeking advice from the one who has been appointed to be in charge of the cellblock or dormitory that they live in. This is the way that the MB's kept organized among themselves, always keeping someone in charge so that order would always exist where they were at. In making some decisions, some produced good fruit, whereas others altered some brother's movements for the rest of their lives, as was demonstrated in the 1993 takeover of the maximum-security prison at Lucasville, Ohio on Easter day. In that takeover, a few brothers were sentenced to death along with some members of the Aryan Brotherhood for supposedly participating in the order to kill a guard.

This is one of the many stories about how the MB's dwell in some state penitentiaries under the same roof with enemies, white supremacist groups, the organizations, homosexuals, plus good and bad prison guards, for years at a time.

All Muslim communities in the penitentiary are not alike; the constitutions, treaties, and the brothers that govern them bring their own unique style in the way that they govern their community. One aspect that is common among all the Sunni Muslims though, the belief that there is no Lord, but Allah and that Prophet Muhammad (pbuh) is the seal of the prophets.

The penitentiary is a world within itself, it's real, volatile and has a diverse group of mentalities forced to live together. The Muslims had to develop security systems to help them run their world. The emergence of intelligence gathering became a natural response to the devious mentalities within the environment that was working to thwart the programs that the Muslims would engage in to advance their way of life.

Brothers had to adopt more than one name at times, develop codes of secrecy just to move around saboteurs of legitimate enterprises.

Instead of presenting a fact by fact analysis of prison statistics or a psychological evaluation of how brothers got into the penitentiary in the first place; the process of dialogue and interaction with the environment will be presented while the MB's practice their way of life.

Being that the prisons in North America contain a large number of black men from the outer society, this is the group that Al-Islam has touched more than any other ethnic group within the penitentiary and continues to do so, It's from this perspective that this is presented.

CHAPTER 1

TRANSITION

"So you want to be a Muslim, huh? Well, since this is the middle of the week, you a be right on time for our orientation class tonight, then we'll hook you up with a pass for our religious services that we call, Jummah."

"What's the orientation class about?"

"Well, young brother, we talk about the basics of what our way of life is all about. We teach a brother how to perform his prayers, so that he can endure the onslaught of negativity that he has to deal with everyday. Then eventually, we'll teach you some Arabic."

"Why Arabic?"

"You see, when you learn how to read that, then you can read our book called the Holy Quran, but don't worry about that right now, it's almost <u>count time</u>. I'll see you on the yard during the recreation period, and then we'll talk some more."

The prison yard, spacious, well kept grass from the constant attention it receives from the laborers at work everyday. A large racetrack to help ease the tension accumulated from the stress of overcrowding in the cellblocks and dormitories. Towers that are built up around high barbed wire fences, which made a person think that they're a prison of war or in a concentration camp. There's also an empty spot that once held thousands of pounds of weight lifting material before the weights were taken out in response to the riot that took place at the maximum security prison in Lucasville, Ohio.

On the prison yard, Abdul Muntaqim, a thirty-five year old brother who is in charge of security for one of the Islamic communities within the penitentiary, was sent to investigate who the new brother is that wanted to come into their ranks.

"Excuse me, my brother, are you the one who was wanting to know something about Al-Islam?" asked Abdul Muntaqim.

"Yeah, that was me," replied Boo, who is twenty-six years old and wants to change his life around. He is a member of the Black Gangster Disciples, a group who no longer calls itself a gang, but an organization. "I was talkin' to one of the brothers earlier and he said that he'll meet me on the yard after count time."

"First of all, my name is Abdul Muntaqim, I'm head of security for our community which we call, Masjid Jihad, and what's your name?"

"They call me, Boo, and I ain't no ghost."

"Yeah, I seen you around the joint before. Tell me Boo, why do you want to become a Muslim right now?"

"Well, Abdul, I'm tired man. Nothin' is workin' for me right now. I look around and guys are getting their heads split over the littlest thing. Things just seem to be getting out of control, I mean, I ain't one that run from trouble, and I'm definitely not goin' to check in."

Abdul Muntaqim nodded his head, implying that he understands what is gong on. "I can understand where you're coming from, Boo. The Muslim community is like an umbrella. It'll provide a brother some shade from the drama that we have to face everyday. Look at Sonny, Bear, Big Ronnie, and Jojo, you remember how they were before they came into the community."

"Yeah, I remember."

"They had inmates terrorized around here, plus they stayed strapped everywhere they went. Look at them now, Boo, they're making five prayers a day, they don't sell dope anymore, and they don't mess with those boys anymore. They even know how to read the Holy Quran in Arabic, now."

"Muntaqim, you're the second one that mentioned somethin' about readin' the Quran in Arabic. I can barely write English, so how about that?"

"Don't worry about not knowing how to read, Boo. We have those in our education department, whose job is to teach a brother how to reach and write better than what they can now."

"Man, I ain't never had any brothers wantin' to show me how to learn somethin' and they don't even know me, like you talkin' about doin' now."

"Check this out, Boo. There are plenty of brothers in that type of situation; they get motivated, finish up high school, go to college and end up with their degrees in here with us."

Abdul Muntaqim changed the subject and got back to his original purpose, who is Boo and what is he about.

"Boo, let me ask you a question."

"What's up?"

"Do you owe anybody any money or are you in trouble right now for anything?" Muntaqim stopped in the middle of the track and looked in Boo's eyes to wait for an answer.

"Wa, what you ask me somethin' like that for, I ain't weak!"

"Well, it's like this, Boo. If you become associated with us, your business becomes our business, so if you're in trouble or debt, we have to get that old baggage squashed right now."

"Okay, I see what you mean."

"If we don't address the past now Boo, we might have to deal with a situation and someone can get hurt when you come into the community."

"Thas what you mean by old baggage; negative things that I was into."

"Exactly Boo. We as Muslims are obligated to protect your wealth, honor, and blood. You have to remember, that we're not on the outside. If something happens here, it has to be dealt with here. We don't want to be caught in a situation where we got to be in the same room with an enemy, who's trying to bust us in the head when we go to sleep, we just won't take that chance, Boo."

While emphasizing his point to Boo, Abdul Muntaqim looked around to make sure the two brothers that he assigned to trail him were in sight.

Boo is unaware of the two brothers on security that's following them. This is the way the Muslim brothers move; watching each others back at all times. This is a serious redemption, everything is about business, even in recreations, and life is just too short. Those that don't stick together are the ones who won't survive.

"Check this scenario out, Boo. What if we're walking on the yard and suddenly someone sneaks up from behind you and hit you in the head with a pipe. We, as Muslims, are not going to let that go without a response."

"Uh, huh."

"If you would have told us from the beginning that somebody might be coming after you because of something that you done in the past, we could have possibly squashed the situation for you."

"You mean sort a like that time those racist bitches jumped on that young brother." Boo clenched his fists because if there's one thing that will bring all the black inmates together on, is too shut down a group of racists.

"That's right, brother," said Abdul Muntaqim.

"But he wasn't no Muslim, though."

Abdul Muntaqim chuckled. "You're right, Boo, he wasn't part of our community, but in actuality, everything is a Muslim, I'll explain that to you some other time though. You see, Boo, we were thinking ahead. If we didn't intervene when we did, there would have been a race war in here, which would have drawn us into it and there would have been some blood for real."

"So you saying that ya'll try to stop things before they happen."

"Exactly Boo. We prefer to negotiate through a situation and if that fails, well, we have a saying that goes like this; Allah knows best."

Boo was referring to a situation where four older members of the so-called Aryan Brotherhood (AB) jumped on a teenage inmate. This group promotes themselves as being superior to all other races; white supremacists. Instead of allowing a free for all, among the black inmates to take revenge, the Emam, came up with "Operation Counteract," to thwart the aggressive movements of the AB. All the black groups were pulled together; the Crips, Bloods, Black Hebrews, Folks, and Muslims, to stop the AB in their tracks.

Abdul Muntaqim continued his conversation with Boo on the yard.

"You see Boo, we understand, as Muslims that if you come into Al-Islam wholeheartedly, and strive to fulfill your obligations, Allah promises to forgive you of the bad things that happened in the past. Now how many of us don't need that Boo?"

"Man, you ain't never lied about that." Boo listened intently to what was being said. He never was told that his past bad deeds could be forgiven a statement that gave him a ray of hope for something better in the future.

"Everybody don't understand that principle Boo, that's why we stay vigilant."

"Hold up. What do you mean vigilant?"

"It means to be watchful, Boo. Like I was saying, it's still those in society as well as in here, that feels that once you fall you're through for life. That's why Al-Islam is appealing to brothers like ourselves, it tells us that we can redeem ourselves once we get on the right path."

"Hey, tell me this, Muntaqim. If I become a Muslim, what am I supposed to do?"

"Before we get into that, my brother, my job is to see who it is that's getting ready to come into our midst, that's why I usually approach a brother to find out who and what he's about. So this is nothing personal, Boo, this is the procedure that I have to follow. The brothers that make up Masjid Jihad makes the rules for every duty that we perform, plus it's in our constitution."

"See there you go again, you went over my head with that one."

"It's like this, Boo. We just don't do what we want to do in here; we have a whole system of conduct that's available to us through the Holy Quran and our books of law."

"So this is where you get what you call a constitution."

"Yeah, that's right, Boo. Everything that we do or attempt to do is based on those books. Things may not turn out the way that we planned, but the intention has a lot to do with it." Abdul Muntaqim scanned the yard as the recreation period began to wind down.

"Boo, this is my job; to be watchful of who comes among the Muslim community. We've seen in the past, how infiltrators came among us which called themselves Muslims, they're whole intention was to undermine the positive things that we were trying to accomplish. But now, Boo, we can't afford to let it happen again and when we expose them, they'll probably get their head split like a pigs foot."

"That's a hard line ain't it, Muntaqim?"

"The bottom line is this, Boo. We're not going for infiltrators, or the one's that we call snitches. When you study history, Boo, you'll understand why we take a hard line like that."

"If I want to be a Muslim, what do I do. I'm talking about right now."

"Well, you would first say, I bear witness that there is no Lord but Allah, and Prophet Muhammad (pbuh) is his Messenger. You would say that in front of two Muslims within the community."

"That's all I gotta do?" Boo asked.

"It's really just the beginning, Boo, that's the part you say with your mouth. There's also actions that you have to perform along with what you said."

"Like what?" Boo asked.

"I'm not going into any details because another brother will be going into that, but I can say this, you'll have to go to orientation first."

"What we gonna do there?"

"Learn how to pray and then learn some Arabic, then we'll hook you up with a pass to come to our prayer services that we call Jummah. Oh, you'll also be expected to send out some charity to a Mosque on the street."

"We barely make enough money for ourselves how we gonna send some money out there?"

"It's easy to do, Boo. A brother just have to stop being selfish and remove some of that stiff necked pride that developed in a brothers system all these years."

"I can't change overnight, Muntaqim, it's goin' to take some time."

"We take you up under our wing and won't let you go, until you can stand on your own. This way you won't be able to go back to doing some of the things that you used to do because you have time. One last thing, young brother, we also have a mandatory workout on the weekend, the workout is designed to keep us strong in unity and spirit." Abdul Muntaqim broke off the conversation. "I got to go brother. I have to meet some brothers."

"So you movin' like that, huh, Muntaqim?"

"It's all in the program, Boo. You'll see what I mean when you get with us."

Back in the dormitories and cellblocks, the MB's always had someone in charge of the other brothers that live there with them. The one most knowledgeable of the Holy Quran and the laws of Islam, is the one who is usually in charge. When it comes to making the final decisions concerning Muslim affairs within these housing units, the brothers must have a record of making sound judgements at a time when emotions may be running high within the dormitory. If a MB gets into a dispute and the senior brother says, "Leave it alone," there's not supposed to be anything else said about the situation until things calm down.

Boo went back to the dorm where about ten MB's live. On the way in, he saw a brother that he knew by the name of Abdul Raheem, a twenty-eight year old brother that runs the public relations department for Masjid Jihad. His job is to make sure that the community's bulletin board is always up to date with Islamic events and news.

"What's up, Raheem?" asked Boo.

"How are you doing, Boo? Everything all right?"

"Yeah, I'm all right. I just got through talking to Muntaqim, he gave it up, I want to learn about Islam."

"That's good to hear, my brother, are you still with the Gangster Disciples?"

"It's time for me to look at somethin' to improve my life, I know that it's time to look at somethin' else."

"Yeah, I can understand that, Boo. What dorm are you in anyway?"

"C Dorm. Why, whas up?"

"Praise due to Allah, you in the same dorm with some high powered brothers. Abdul Hakeem is the brother that you want to see when you go back."

"How come all of ya'll don't get into the same dorms and blocks together Raheem, that way yawl can control it."

"Well, we prefer to be spread out for a couple of reasons. For one, it gives us a better opportunity to teach more brothers, plus you know how volatile things can get at the spur of the moment, right?"

"Right."

"Being spread out is a good strategic move. With brothers in every dorm and block, means that we'll always be informed about everything that happens around here."

Boo nodded his head in agreement. "Yeah, I see what you mean."

"Are you going to lunch today, Boo?"

"I got to have it, man, whatever it is, except that pork. My locker box is on empty right now. I mean, I can easily make some money and keep my pockets fat, but I ain't tryin' to move like that anymore."

"That's a good start, Boo, to know what's been holding you back."

"As soon as I get into the game, it seems like negative consequences start to follow, that's why I got to get another way of life."

"You know, Boo, if you're sincere about wanting to change, our community has things set up for a brother like yourself who is trying to change.

Some of us came from that same situation. We came out of the gangster life, taking what we wanted and not caring about the consequences."

"I know that you didn't move like that, Raheem, I mean that you don't look like you have the personality to indulge in too much wrong."

"That's where Al-Islam came in at, Boo, I'm in the make over stage now. It took a little time to get rid of some of those destructive habits and it's still a struggle."

Every month the brothers contribute to a fund to help out inmates who come into the religion and have to start all over with nothing.

"What we have is this, Boo. We have all the brothers within the community give something in the way of shoes, sweat suits, socks, soap, and deodorant to start a brother off when he need something."

"So you sayin', Raheem, that this will help a brother get away from the crazy stuff to get what he need and that the Muslim brothers will help him to get what he needs."

"Exactly, Boo, it's like a tax to us in here. Even though you and I know that there's cash money floating around here, we try to stay away from it because it's a risk to handle it. We use tangible items like those I just mentioned as a way of paying taxes and as giving charity at the same time."

"The crew that I'm in, we really never moved on that level, you know, the tax thing."

"Boo, when you start to come into a higher understanding of how society runs itself and how the government runs itself, we can start to apply some of those same ideas to our situation and survive among ourselves."

"So what we do, Raheem, is take what we can that is useful and leave off the other stuff."

"You're catching on, Boo. The same thing goes for something to eat. If you are hungry, I am hungry. We call it the principle of wanting for your brother, what you want for yourself. It can be canned goods, zoo-zoo's, or wam-wams. The bottom line is that you are not going without, even in this situation, Boo."

"Do we have to pay any of that back, Raheem?"

"We don't look at it as brothers getting paid back, Boo, we look at it as being your community now, so you'll be giving back to yourself.

You will understand those principles down the road, it's all about taking one step at a time."

"Did all the brothers start out with ya'll givin' them somethin' to get on their feet, Raheem?"

"Nawl, Boo, some brothers already came in the penitentiary with their situation straight; they just had to do this time, that's all."

"I was always wonderin' how come the MB's always have somethin' goin' on in the way of business, that's because ya'll look out for each other."

"That's what we try to do, Boo. If we didn't have the Holy Quran and the acts of the Prophet Muhammad (pbuh) to check our conduct, we'd be in the same type of gangster mind now, as we did when we came in here."

"Do everybody in the dorms and the cellblocks start out the same, when ya'll set 'em up?"

"Every brother is given the opportunity to run their own store. The zoo-zoo's, wams and the whole works, except that dope game. A brother is going to have some trouble from us if we find out he's doing that."

"It's plenty of that, too Raheem." Boo knows for sure because he wants to get out of the game.

"Once a brother has all that store business out the way, he can better concentrate on his Islamic studies and strive to get some piece of mind, while fighting to get out of here; in the meantime, we're all family, Boo."

"Ya'll ain't the only family, though Raheem."

"You're right about that, Boo, but we can say that we're a family that base our actions on a moral context within the penitentiary. Think about what some of those other groups base their families on, Boo."

"That is a good point, Raheem, there is something missing."

"What's missing, Boo, is the revelation from Allah, that's what's missing. Something that gives a brother a sense of fulfillment in his life; not somethin' based on cutting your throat."

"Wait a minute, Raheem yawl cracked some heads before, too, so how do you explain that one?"

"You right, Boo, but we don't go around being the aggressor in our actions. The Holy Quran says that Allah is not with the aggressor, and we believe that!, we are not going to turn no other cheek, either. We cannot go hide in here when things happen; something is in your face everyday; from the crack, to the bozo, and the boys, we have to keep pressing, my brother, we call it jihada, exerting ourselves to fight against the vices."

"What can I say, Raheem, this is all new to me, but it sounds proper, I'm gonna make me a transition, how you say it, if it please, Allah."

CHAPTER 2

CELLBLOCKS, DORMITORIES, CHOW HALL

Once recreation is over with, inmates have to report to their living quarters, which is either a cellblock or dormitory. Everything in the penitentiary is based upon time. Everyone's movement is clocked; if an inmate is not in the place where he is supposed to be when count time begins; it can cause a disruption among the thousands of inmates that exist within that particular system. When the count is delayed, inmates can be locked down for hours until the right count is presented.

Abdul Raheem and Boo made it back to their dorms on time. In these dorms, everything is in the open for everyone to see, which causes stress because you can rarely relax. In the animal world, if certain animals are caught napping, they can become another animal's next meal.

That same type of tendency to victimize or destroy others for one's own benefit, exist when a person is perceived as weak or wounded. Going to sleep at night and then waking up in the morning through each of the seasons and then looking into the same deadly stares of inmates everyday, can be traumatic.

"What are you staring at me for?"

"I ain't lookin' at you, man, I just woke up." Pretty soon, inmates learn how to move around making eye contact with other inmates so as not to be perceived as a threat. Depending on where the bed is located within the dorm, there could be someone sleeping on all sides of you including on top or bottom of the bunk.

When Boo got back to the dorm, he immediately looked for Abdul Hakeem, a forty two year old brother who acts in the capacity of a consultant to the younger brothers in Masjid Jihad. Boo was so thrilled about finding out about a new way of life, that he bypassed his own bed and locker box to find Hakeem. Before he reached his destination, one of his associates that he was trying to break free from, had stopped him.

"Whas up, Boo?" said Tone, a twenty five year old member of the Black Gangster Disciples. "What are you into, my folks?"

"Hey, Tone, what's been up with you?"

"You know what it's about, Boo, making money any way that we can as long as we can and it don't stop in here," Tone stared in Boo's eyes, but didn't see the usual enthusiastic response that he normally got from Boo. "I see that you been kickin' it with the MB's real tough lately, what about us, your family?"

"I been tryin' to find out some things thas all." Tone put his colored handkerchief on the bed rail as if to remind Boo of what he's supposed to be about; a Black Gangster Disciple. He then threw up a hand sign in the form of the letter F that stands for Folks. The name, Folks, covers all the sets or groups of gangsters that identify with the six pointed star. "You know we stand on the six point star Boo.

This what we about, you can never forget that." The six pointed star, as opposed to the five pointed star, that's used with the moon in some Islamic nations flags has become a point of contention in some of the organizations philosophy because of some misunderstandings about what the points may mean.

Being that the influence of Al-Islam is strong within the prison system, a large number of those who were once in the organizations or gangs, are often attracted to the symbolism, colors, and flags with these symbols upon them.

The Islamic Hebrews have a six pointed star, therefore when the gangsters see that symbol, they begin to inquire of the Muslims who may wear the ring ,asking what is it all about and then they begin to be taught Al-Islam.

The five pointed star surrounded by the moon, with the color red in it, attracts members of the blood organizations and others from other groups who go through different transformations before settling on what group of Muslims they want to belong to.

They might be attracted to the Nation of Islam, Five Percenters, the Muslim American Society, the Islamic Hebrews, the Moorish Science community, or one of the communities with the traditional four schools of thought.

Colors and symbolism is what first attracts some inmates to the various Islamic communities. Some inmates are so entrenched into these colors and stars that it often blocks off their communication with other people because a person might be wearing red or blue.

After Boo had been reminded about that which he was supposed to be about as a gangster, he responded by backing up from the bed and gave Tone a stare. "I mean, so what if I'm kickin' it with the Muslims? Did I do somethin' wrong or what?"

"No, Boo," replied Tone. "There ain't nothing wrong with that, i'm just wondering how come you ain't been coming around like you used to do."

"Look here, Tone, I know that we're gangsters. I'm just tryin' to see if there's somethin' more meaningful than what I been doing so far." Boo hit his chest to emphasize how strong he feels about the issue. "I'm goin' to tell you now, Tone, if I'm going to do something, I'm gonna do it."

"You in the penitentiary, Boo. You can't get away from nothing in here unless you go and check in." Boo didn't respond and walked away. "I'm gonna talk with you later Boo," shouted Tone.

Boo walked through the rows of beds where inmates must spend years at a time, either using their time productively or planning on how to further their criminal career.

Boo walked to the back of the dorm where Abdul Hakeem and four other MB's were. "Hakeem, what's up?" he said.

"Under the circumstances, I'm well, young brother. All praise is due to Allah. What can I do for you?" replied the seasoned consultant to Islamic community.

"I was on the yard talkin' to Muntaqim a little earlier about learning somethin about Islam." That statement caught the attention of the other brothers sitting around. "He told me to come and see you."

"Yeah, I did get word that you would be coming. So you want to learn about this religion huh?" said Hakeem.

"That's why I came to see you. I want to start at the beginning and take my time and learn as much as I can because I heard that it was a lot to learn."

"Well, Boo, that's the duty of every Muslim, to pass on the knowledge, it's one of our six points," said Abdul Hakeem. Boo listened attentively, seeing older brothers with some strength and talking sense instead of how they used to sell dope or pimp before they came into the penitentiary.

"This is what I'm going to do right now, Boo. I'm going to finish talking with these brothers. I might as well introduce you to them. This is Abdul Salaam, he's the one who calls all the brothers to pray with his voice."

"Yeah, I hear him in the mornin' sometimes, and it seems like he be singin' or somethin'." Hakeem finished the introductions. "This is Abdul Samee, Kareem, and Rasool."

"How ya'll brothers doin'?" said Boo.

"All praise is due to Allah, we're breathing, young brother."

"I'll get back with you in the day room, Boo, I got to finish up this business for now."

"When we gonna do that, after count or what?"

"Yeah, we'll get together after count."

Abdul Hakeem and the brothers constantly get together so that they can stay on top of everything that goes on within the dormitory, as well as the penitentiary at large. The unity that they display has an effect upon other inmates and becomes a silent teaching tool within itself.

The day room is a room that the MB's use to perform their congregational prayers together; other inmates iron their clothes or lounge around, or some go to just get away from the overcrowded dorm.

Abdul Hakeem met Boo in the day room. "Well, well, well, so you want some knowledge, huh, Boo?" asked Abdul Hakeem, as he sat down at the table with his black fez on his head.

"Yeah it's that time, Hakeem. I'm twenty six and I got eight more years to go before I get out of here so I got to get myself together."

"Becoming a Muslim is a big step in your life, Boo because there's a lot to learn. We got a saying that goes like this, "Seek knowledge from the cradle to the grave." All Muslims are taught that, Boo, learning never stops, you should do it for the rest of your life."

Boo are all ears, he never heard some of these sayings before.

"You got any questions so far, Boo?"

"I been watchin' ya'll for the past couple of months and I know that I can do those things, even getting' up early in the mornin' there's just one thing that I got to take care of first."

"What's that, Boo?"

"You know that I'm a gangster. I'm goin' to have to work it out with them."

"I already know who you're rolling with Boo. I see the handshakes and the kind of handkerchief that you and Tone usually exchange. So it's no surprise that you're going to have to tell them. We'll let the security department handle the situation along with you, we've dealt with this type of thing plenty of times."

"Ya'll did?"

"Boo, come on, you think that you're the only gangster that came to the religion? Brothers from all walks of life are coming all the time."

"Now, that's what I'm talkin' about. I never see any punks in ya'll ranks, either."

"You never will, Boo. Only Allah knows what's in a person's heart, so we can't make any judgement on that, but we can say this. If a homosexual comes into our ranks, he won't stay that way long because we're going to drive him until he won't have time to be with another man."

"So ya'll work on em, huh, Hakeem?"

"You got that right, Boo. All the way from the teachings telling him to be a man, to our workouts of boxing, running, and wrestling. All that will bring the man out of him."

"You know that they be sayin' that they born like that."

"I'm not goin' into all that, Boo. I want to tell you about some of these principles of Al-Islam. We're going to start you with the basics, we call them the five pillars."

"Why you call them pillars, Hakeem?"

"A pillar is something that stands for support and those five pillars is what you'll stand upon to take you to a higher understanding in your life."

"I'm startin' to feel better already just talkin' about somethin' positive, how about a name though Hakeem?

Wait a minute, young brother, you have to slow down, you're going to burn yourself out like a shooting star if you move too fast."

"Yeah, I hear you, man, I'm just excited from what I'm starting to hear, that's all."

"You're supposed to get excited, but we have to show you how to channel that energy so that it won't be wasted on foolishness anymore."

"Well I got time to learn and that's for sure."

"You're right, Boo. You do have time, it seems like time stops in here, but it doesn't, I got six more years to do and I'm staying busy every moment."

"Me and you might be getting out the same time, Hakeem."

"Boo, if you study and have some patience, you'll be able to go a long way. What I mean by that is the ignorance, lack of understanding, and disregard for life that's been in you for all these years can be replaced with some strong decent principles."

"That's a lot to do, man, because I been a gangster all of my life, well, since I was eight years old."

"Let me say this, Boo. The knowledge of Islam can take a person that's beat down, misused, ignorant, and considered a throw away by society and make a better person out of him. We can think of Malcolm X as a prime example. He came from the streets, went to the penitentiary and became influenced by the teachings of Elijah Muhammad."

"You got any books about Malcolm X, Hakeem? I wanna' read something about him."

"I see that you're starting to get hungry already, Boo, and that's good."

"Didn't the old Nation break up sometime ago? I hear about that on the yard sometimes."

"I see, but you're definitely right Boo, the original Nation of Islam was disbanded by Elijah Muhammad's son, Emam W.D. Mohammed, in order to take his followers into what's called a Sunni Muslims way of life."

"What was that word again?"

"Sunni, that's what I am. It means following the path of the last prophet sent to the world called Prophet Muhammad (pbuh)."

"I never heard that part, Hakeem, you gonna have to tell me somethin' about who he was, but who run the Nation of Islam now?"

"Of course, you've heard of Minister Farrakhan. Remember the Million-Man March? Well he started it up again."

"Okay. Let me ask you somethin' else."

"Go right ahead, young brother, that's what I'm here for."

"What do your name mean?"

"Well, Boo, it's what we call an attribute of Allah. One of his ninety-nine names. The one that I have is one that a brother helped me to pick, It was about ten years ago when I first came to the penitentiary."

"Yeah, but what do it mean though?"

"Hakeem means the wise one, but Allah is the ultimate wise one, so we refer to him as, The Wise. Now as far as I'm concerned, I'm just Abdul Hakeem, which means the servant of the wise one."

"So the word, Abdul, should go in front of your name?"

"You catch on quick, young brother, you may not hear brothers say the word, Abdul, all the time, but technically it should go in front of any attribute of Allah. Not to cut this off too short, Boo, but it's just about lunch time, are you going?"

"No doubt, they having that macaroni cheese, and fish."

"It's about time they serve some fish again, that means it's going to be crowded in the cafeteria this afternoon, you want to ride with us?"

"Yeah, why not?"

"You know that Tone and the other gangsters are going to be watching you."

"I got to move on, Hakeem, but I aint going to disrespect anybody. I'm gonna talk to all of 'em real soon."

When inmates do any moving around in the penitentiary, they must carry around an identification badge. The badges have the inmate's race, weight, height, date of birth, and thumb print on one side and then the inmate's picture on the other side. Without this badge, it'll be difficult to transact any penitentiary business or move around without being stopped by the guards.

Abdul Hakeem and the other brothers have headgear that's worn wherever they go. The right to wear their fezzes and other headgear was won through hard fought battles in the courts of the land. There have been many brothers who have gone to the hole after they have been granted the right to wear them, because of those authorities who have been hesitant to change in spite of what the law said.

As times began to change and more prison personnel become better acquainted with different lifestyles than what they were brought up with, there have been less problems with what brothers wear on their heads.

As lunchtime approached the brothers got together. "Are you going to lunch, Abdul Salaam?" asked Hakeem.

"You know it, brother, I need those potatoes and broccoli in my system, I'm trying to bulk up."

"Check and see if the other brothers are ready yet, I'm going to get Boo. We'll let him ride with us for awhile, this way he can get a feel of how we move, plus we can see how he reacts to the gangsters watching him."

Abdul Hakeem walked to Boo's bed with his beard trimmed and shoes polished to see if he's ready. "Let's go, Boo, they're serving fish and you can leave that handkerchief here because the administration is getting ready to take all of those anyway, so you might as well get used to it."

"Oh that's what you heard, huh?" asked Boo.

"Yeah, Boo. They want to break up anything that dare to call themselves an organization around here."

"Let's go get some food, Hakeem. I ain't even gonna worry about those kind of things anymore. Cosmo should have some extra fish for us for a couple of packs of cigarettes."

"Good looking, Boo, but you know that we're going to get ours, we got brothers working in the kitchen, that way we make sure we'll eat. You got to realize, Boo, we've been organized in these penitentiaries for a long time. That's why you'll find the Muslims involved in almost every area of the penitentiary."

"So ya'll get into somethin' to take it over, huh?"

"Not so much as that, Boo. We just don't believe in being on the outside looking in. We believe in being on the inside and controlling our own affairs."

Boo has never been around brothers that been talking about politics, going inside of an organized body, and working from there. "Hakeem, what about that lard thing?"

"Man, you popping questions out of the clear blue, your mind must be starting to click, Boo."

"I'm startin' to think different too. I mean, I know that I can't change overnight, but I'm startin' to think about ways of doin' things in life a little different than what I was doin'."

"About that lard. Boo, in Al-Islam, we say that you are what you eat, meaning that you can be affected internally and externally by what you take in your body. You see how alcohol can change your behavior when you drink?"

"Yeah."

"Well, foods do the same thing. It's just that the average person can't tell how foods affect their mental and physical being because they don't know themselves. I'm really going to show you about that swine and all the things that it's made from."

"Buy my mama and grandma still eat pork and they doin' alright. As a matter of fact, Grandma eats chitlins once in awhile."

Abdul Hakeem noticed that Boo's voice crackled a little when he mentioned his mother, so he makes sure that he stays away from talking about her and just deals with the issue. Inmates try to stay away from emotionally charged issues because it affects the hardness that has to be developed in order to cope with an often-harsh reality, the penitentiary.

"Check this out, Boo. I understand where you're coming from. A lot of us came up eating foods that was harmful to us, but now we know the difference between what's lawful and what's not, remember how those chitlins used to smell?"

"Yeah, they did smell pretty bad, though."

"One thing is for sure, Boo, I never did eat any."

"Let's go to lunch, Hakeem, I'm hungry talkin' about any kind of food." Abdul Hakeem, Boo, and the rest of the brothers go through the narrow door of the dormitory designed in such a way that only one inmate can get through at a time, another way to make sure that inmates are controlled in their movements.

All the Muslims wear their fezzes or other headgear at the present time. They're the only group of inmates that can be found wearing some type of religious head wear, unless it's some Jews, which one rarely sees.

Inmates wearing baseball caps, scarves, or any other type of head wear that doesn't have a religious affiliation to it, cannot wear those items in the classrooms, chow hall, library, or offices of prison employees as the Muslims can with their head wear. With that privilege, the Muslims safeguard it by making sure that no one abuses it. There are times when an inmate will come across a fez and put it on, the Muslims will approach him and ask him not to wear it. Sometimes the request will work and once in awhile a more forceful approach will have to be advanced.

The MB's try to do everything in unity; eating, praying, studying, and going to recreation all together. In an atmosphere of hardness, which some penitentiaries consist of more than others, having unity and strength is conducive to the growth of the spirit and moral well being of individual brothers.

The narrow hallway to the chow hall provides another example of the way prison officials plan in case of an emergency. The ceilings have metal gates that can drop down to the floor by the push of a button, in order to break up a large number of inmates into groups of twenty to thirty, if the occasion arises.

On their way to chow, Abdul Hakeem and Boo met up with some other brothers from B Block. The majority of inmates try their best to get into the cellblocks because of the privacy that a brother can get from them. Brothers in the cellblocks can usually perform their prayers in their cells and once in awhile perform them together at the back of the block.

"As-salaam alaikum believers," said Abdul Muntaqim, as he and five other brothers from B Block met up with Abdul Hakeem in the hallway.

"Wa-alaikum salaam, how's all the brothers this afternoon?" asked Abdul Hakeem.

"Ah, I see that you caught up with Boo, " Abdul Muntaqim said to him.

"I'm just tryin' to learn somethin' about Islam," Boo said excitedly, as he noticed members of the Gangster Disciples coming his way.

"Hey, G, we got to talk with you, how about later on?" shouted out Tone. Abdul Muntaqim took notice of the conversation and detected some animosity towards Boo

."What's going on young Boo? What's wrong with them?"

"They heard that I want to be a Muslim, now they tryin' to say that I just can't go out like that."

"Man, this is Al-Islam!" shouted Abdul Muntaqim. "If a person wants to come this way, nobody can stop them, if they try to, we gonna ride on 'em."

Emam Maleek walked up, he's in the same block as Abdul Muntaqim, his head of security.

"As-salaam alaikum, believers, what's going on here?"

"Wa-alaikum salaam, brother Emam," answered all the brothers.

"This is Boo right here," said Abdul Muntaqim, pointing him out to the Emam. "I was just telling him that no one can stop him from coming into this way of life."

"That's right, no one can stop you from coming into this way of life, but what's all this loud talk about that I heard when I walked up?" Emam Maleek has dealt with this type of situation before and knows what to do. "What are they trying to say that you can't get out, Boo?"

"Yeah, I can get out, It's just how I come out, that's the problem, they want six boxes of cigarettes."

Abdul Muntaqim stepped in the conversation furious. "We ain't paying for nobody so that they can be in this religion!"

"Just relax, brother," said the Emam. "This might be the way to free this slave. I think that we can work something out to avoid conflict because those that we may disagree with today, can be our greatest allies tomorrow. Let me come up with something."

When the Emam usually finished with a matter, that would usually be the end of the conversation, but Abdul Muntaqim still wants to check them.

"Let me and the brothers go and check them, brother Emam."

"I already spoke on it, brother, now let's go and get something to eat.

Boo just keep your eyes and ears open. If you notice, we have two ears and one mouth, the Messenger of Allah may the peace and blessings of Allah be upon him said, that two things will get you into hell fire if misused, your tongue and private parts."

"I don't understand, " said Boo.

"That's why I be on brothers to guard what they say because it can get them in trouble. The least little thing said around here can be interpreted wrong. Plus, look at all those homosexuals around here.

You'll never find them in our ranks. Every time you look around, one of them have Kool-Aid on their lips and cheeks trying to look like a woman. That's why I instruct the head of security to be hard on brothers when they start to get weak and drift around those boys, unless it's about strictly business."

When the brothers finally reached the chow hall, there were two lines that they had a choice to stand in to get their food. One of the lines is where the majority of black and Latino inmates sit down and eat while the other line is where the white inmates eat. This is career out of this and that's for real."

"Yeah, I know what you mean, it do pay the bills though."

"This place is really hazardous to a man's health, plus I do not want to be around here when things start to explode."

"Don't worry about that, Johnson because if something do happen, we'll make sure that we remember those that treated us right. One thing is for sure, you always treated us with respect, and that counts for a lot up in this penitentiary."

Abdul Muntaqim finally went to Omar's cell and knocked on the door before looking in. The cellblock is the last area of privacy within the penitentiary that an inmate can go to.

Omar is the assistant Emam; he's thirty-eight years old and has been locked up for twelve years. Before coming into Islam, he had killed two dope dealers because of a bad dope deal.

"As-salaam alaikum, believer. What's going on up this way?" asked Muntaqim.

"Wa-alaikum salaam, my brother. I'm good. All praise is due to Allah, he blessed me to wake up this morning to make my prayers so I'm all right."

"I'm just passing through to let you know that the Emam wants to have a meeting for all the department heads after the class. If there is any concerns that has to be presented, you can do it then."

"One thing about me, brother," said Omar, as he brushed off his black velvet fez. "I been doing these meetings for about eight years in here so I know what to expect."

While Muntaqim and Omar discuss the up and coming class, Ronnie Muhammad, a twenty five year old brother on security, walked up. When asked about his mood while doing his time, he always says that it's fearing Allah and exerting himself in the cause of Al-Islam.

"As-salaam alaikum, believers," said Muhammad, walking up on the brothers as close as possible and extending his hands.

"Wa-alaikum salaam, Muhammad," replied Abdul Muntaqim. "I see that you're on the move as usual."

"Just keeping those in check who need to be checked, you know how I like it, I got to stay in the mix for the pleasure of Allah."

"Ain't no mystery brother," said Abdul Muntaqim, as he put his hand on Muhammad's shoulder. "How's your store going?"

"All praise is due to Allah, it's keeping me from doing something wrong around here the way inmates prefer to have it, to be among their own group.

The lines are referred to as the white line and black line. There are those who are in the white supremacist organizations who has documented papers that says their religion dictates that they shouldn't be in the same cell with anyone black. That type of thinking is carried into every aspect of their stay within the penitentiary with the results being separate lines to stand in and separate tables to eat at.

During the negotiating phase of the deadly riot at the maximum security prison in Lucasville, Ohio, where nine inmates and one guard were killed, one of the demands of the AB was the they didn't want to be forced to live in the same cell with no one but white inmates.

The MB's really didn't care that strongly about who would come into the cell, as long as they respected their way of life. The average black inmate wasn't so strung out on this issue, they usually responded to the situation by grouping up and then demanding the same thing as the white inmates when it came down to it. But there was always a line to be drawn by the prison authorities when it came to black inmates wanting to bunch up together, mainly because of the number of them that existed within the penitentiary.

Back in the cafeteria, Abdul Hakeem and the rest of the MB's finally reached the front of the long line to be served.

"It's the Muslim brothers, no pork, no pork!" shouted out Cosmo, a food line server who is a friend of Boo and Abdul Hakeem. "Salaam salaikum, Hakeem, what's up?"

"No, Cosmos. It's As-salaam alaikum, my brother, everything is good, and all praise is due to Allah. Hook us up with some of that fish," said Abdul Hakeem.

"Let me see, ah, where is that pan that I set aside for ya'll because I'm always gonna look out for the brothers. Hey, I see my dude Boo is with ya'll, what's up man?"

"It's time for me to get serious about some things, Cosmo. I want to learn about what the real life is all about, I'm gonna start goin' to the Islamic classes, why don't you come with me?"

Cosmo opened his eyes up wide and said, "Not yet, Boo. I know that I'm gonna still do a lot of dirt; smoking some of that bozo, and messin' around with those boys once in awhile, no, I can't do it yet, Boo."

"At least you bein' for real man. I'll check with you later at recreation." Some of the other brothers were already sitting down at the tables eating. All of them have either their fezzes or other headgear on. Not all of the brothers are in the same community, but they all share the same area. Besides Masjid Jihad, which Emam Maleek is the head over, there's Masjid Fattah.

The brothers in Masjid Fattah are less tolerant in a number of ways than the brothers in Masjid Jihad. It's not that they're more militant, they just prefer to be more physical, cracking skulls is what they're known for and less talk. Some of the members are extreme in their acts of worship; an example of this is when it's time for the early Morning Prayer, instead of calling the brothers to prayer in a quiet tone, they'll call it out loud without respecting other inmates right to keep sleeping in the early morning in the dormitory, instead of respect, inmates feared them.

Abdul Mumeet, in particular, is a brother that was known throughout the state penitentiaries for what he's about. He's knowledgeable of the Holy Quran and the books which contain the sayings and acts of the Prophet Muhammad (pbuh) but there are those that question his understanding of those books, quietly.

Because of his knowledge, he's able to influence inmates and Muslims wherever he goes. Whoever deals with him, it's done with caution, because of his unpredictability. He was a Muslim on the outer society before coming to the penitentiary, unlike the majority of those inmates who accepted, Al-Islam, while incarcerated. With that background, he brings a different insight which he combines with the prison environment, which at times makes some of his actions seem ruthless to those who don't understand him. In and out of the penitentiary since he was seventeen years old, Abdul Mumeet has done three years here, five there, or six here. Every place that he's been, it always been some blood spilt and he manages to either get away, or do little time that is handed out to him from the internal court system called the Rules Infraction Board (RIB).

The RIB's purpose is to pronounce judgement upon inmates who have supposedly broken prison rules. Sentences can range from fifteen days, months, and even years in an isolated part of the penitentiary, depending on the severity of the penalty.

There are a number of brothers who consider themselves engaged in war, as they do their time within the walls of the penitentiary. With that thinking, everything goes; retribution will be carried out no matter where and when. It can be on the prison yard, in the cafeteria where everyone is watching, to set an example; it doesn't matter where it's at, especially when it came to a MB being threatened.

This was Abdul Mumeet's theater. He was feared before he came to Al-Islam and some of his tactics were carried over to his conversion to the religion. Everything was now carried out in what his understanding of what Islam was all about.

Those who had gotten weak, and strayed away from the religion, and therefore went back to their old ways, stayed vigilant of Abdul Mumeet. It was uncomfortable for them to move in the open, in the tightness of the penitentiary environment, an environment that called for a swiftness of action for any violation of any organization's rules.

Abdul Mumeet's decision was always death when it came to those who either left the religion or wounded a Muslim in a conflict. One thing was for sure though; the MB's would rather have Abdul Mumeet on their side when it came to dealing with any rivals, than be on the other side.

During lunch, Abdul Hakeem and the rest of the brothers were eating one of the same meals that's served every Friday; fish, macaroni and cheese, salad, spinach, and Kool-Aid. The table where Abdul Mumeet, Abdul Muntaqim and other brothers on security are discussing security concerns, Boo is diverted from going near.

"Come over here, Boo, they have business to talk about," said Abdul Hakeem.

"Yeah, I see Mumeet over there, all of 'em looks' real serious, is everything all right?" asked Boo.

"We really don't want to worry about them, Boo, because that's security business. If brother Abdul Muntaqim wants us to know about what's going on, he'll let us know. When we get back to the dorm, there's a basic book on Al-Islam that I'm going to give you, we're going to concentrate on the basics."

"That's just where I want to start, at the beginning, I want to get away from all the negativity that I can."

"I'm going to tell you what else that we're going to work on, Boo."

"What's that?"

"That language of yours brother. We're going to work on some of those words that you're using, I'm going to get you into some Basic English books too."

"I can't forget my roots, Hakeem."

"Yeah, that's understandable, Boo, but that doesn't mean that you have to stay in the slums, brother. Did you graduate from high school?"

"I want to get my, what they call it, GED. All I got to do is sign up for it, that's all."

"We're goin' to help you out, Boo. Don't worry about it."

"That's all I'm lookin' for, Hakeem. Somebody to put me on." Chow time is over and everyone is rushed out of the cafeteria, everything is based on time. Once imitates arrive at their appointed prison to do their time, they're given a little more time to eat than when they first entered the system at what's called the Reception Center. At the Reception Center, all inmates are given about seven minutes to swallow, hide their food, and then get out of the chow hall.

This is where the bitterest against the system began to really hit home; an inmate being locked up twenty three hours of the day with nothing but the walls to look at, one five minute shower every four or five days, a five minute phone call every week, and nothing to read for the first two to four weeks. This is also a period where the most suicidal talk is heard among the weak.

After leaving the chow hall, all the inmates within the state penitentiaries has an assignment that they have to attend to. It may be in the newly thriving penal industries market that has unions in the outer society furious because of the profits and jobs that's been taken away from their own people and given to inmates for slave wages.

There's also school, clerk jobs, maintenance, kitchen duties, and a host of other less than meaningful jobs to keep numerous inmates busy.

Back at C Dorm, where Abdul Hakeem is a barber, Boo works in the laundry room and Abdul Salaam is the clerk of the dorm. These jobs help the inmates to pass the time for them for years at a time.

"I'm going to cut some hair, Salaam," said Hakeem. "You know how these brothers want to look good for the picture project that's coming up tomorrow."

"Yeah, brother, those Jay-Cee's sure do be making some nice money off of us, don't they?" asked Salaam. "But I'm glad that some Muslim brothers in top positions in there because we're going to need their help in getting a new rug to sit on for Islamic services. Who's running the Jay-Cee's anyway?"

"I think its brother, Bashir. He's running it like a top-flight business. They've been making money ever since he took it over."

"Let's see, Hakeem, we got brothers in every inmate program within this joint, except that organization that's named the Steps or something like that."

"You're right, Salaam, because you know what they're about, all of them over there wants to be a Nazi, Klansman, or skin head."

"They do have those swastika's and lightning bolts on their necks and arms, don't they Hakeem?"

"As long as they stay out of our way, because we'll shut 'em down fast, if it ever came down to that. This is the penitentiary; they can't hide in here like they can't on the street. I want you to start working and moving with this, Boo, because we're going to pull him away from those gangs. All he needs is an alternative. As a matter of fact, I want you to start getting him up in the morning, so that he can see the way that we prepare for prayer."

Abdul Salaam rubbed his beard and said, "Do you think he's ready to start getting up that early, brother?"

"We're going to get him ready, brother. That's how a brother comes up strong, by doing it with us. You remember how Ali used to do it, he stayed with you every chance that he got, till it was determined that you can stand and move on your own. Look at you now, two years later, you know fifteen chapters in the Holy Quran by heart and you're also the caller to prayer."

"All praise is due to Allah, Abdul Hakeem. We just got to maintain, brother."

CHAPTER 3

MUSLIM BUSINESS

At B-Block where Emam Maleek and the head of security, Abdul Muntaqim reside, both of these brothers prefer the cells to the dormitories because they are able to perform their prayers in privacy and having some privacy is conducive to a brother's growth in an overcrowded, stressed out situation.

Emam Maleek's present concern is how the meeting of the two security teams from Masjid Jihad and Masjid Fattah came along in their negotiations.

"As-salaam alaika, believer," said the Emam, a thirty five year old brother who has three years left on his sentence before he goes home.

"Wa-alaika salaam, my brother," replied Abdul Muntaqim who then embraced the Emam.

"How did the meeting go with the other community?" asked the Emam.

"Well, we came to an agreement on some of the security issues, but Abdul Mumeet was difficult to deal with as usual, he has a problem with how much information should be exchanged between us."

"What is it this time? It's always something with that brother, but then again I can see why he stays so secretive, look at his background."

"He doesn't object to the joint workouts between the two communities, he's mostly concerned that brothers will find out too much about him, and the way that they operate their security operations."

"Well, if you noticed, " said Maleek, "he and about four other brothers never have taken pictures during our feast after the fast is over like the rest of us, that way no one can ever point to a picture and point him out."

"One thing is for sure," said Muntaqim. "He may have a lot of enemies, but he sure know how to survive all these years in light of all that he's been doing."

"Yeah, my brother," replied the Emam. "If all we disagree on is the way security works, finalize the treaty and emphasize to them that we can still work together when it comes to general threats to our communities."

"So that I understand you right, Emam Maleek, you're saying go ahead with what the treaty says, but don't worry about what Abdul Mumeet is emphasizing about him wanting to stay secret."

"That's it brother, plus I want you to inform the department heads that there will be a meeting after class, and if they have any concerns, present them then."

The meetings that the MB's have help them to maintain their cohesiveness among each other in the penitentiary as a whole. Masjid Jihad's structure is set up where many brothers as possible participate in the communities' affairs. This is done to help prevent brothers from being drawn back into the vice that encloses them on a constant basis. With nowhere to flee, a strong organization is what helps to combat the onslaught of aggressive inmates and vice that permeates the prison society.

Emam (leader)

Assistant Emam

First Amir

  Caller to prayer.

Amir/Head of Security

  Lieutenant

  Sergeant

Amir/Education.

  Instructors

Amir/Finances

  Zakat (charity)

  a. Secretary   b. Stores

"Did you also want to speak to the brothers on security after class, brother Emam?"

"Hmm, we only have two hours and fifteen minutes. I don't know if we can fit it in, but we'll see. By the way Muntaqim, how's your understanding about everyone's position in the community, because you're third in line for leadership so you definitely have to know them all."

"I got an hour before I go to work, brother Emam, you want me to run them down?"

"Yes, brother, but don't get long winded."

"The head of the community is the Emam, he leads us in prayer and protects us with the help of Allah from harm and threat. He has the final say so in matters pertaining to the community after consultation with the members of the community."

"All right, you seem to know about the Emam and what he's appointed to do, who's next?"

"The first Amir, who's also referred to as the Assistant Emam. He stands in the Emam's place when he's not there. He's an intermediator between yourself and the brothers when messages or problems arise at the spur of the moment."

"Okay, stop there. I have no doubt that you know about the other positions, so we can move on from there. I want you to give the speech on Friday, so get ready."

"I have to brush up on my Arabic, especially for the first part because the second half I have down pat."

"I have a visit that day, Muntaqim, plus it's time for you to set up. You have a lot to offer these young brothers that follow your instructions on a daily basis."

"All praise is due to Allah, you got a visit huh!"

Abdul Muntaqim is thrilled to hear about the visit because he and the Emam were good friends before they came to Al-Islam and have been maintaining a closer brotherhood now that they're in the religion together.

"Yeah, brother," said Abdul Maleek. "Kareema's been hanging with me for ten years now. When I first came in here and decided to become a Muslim without hesitation, she said if that's where you can find some peace, then go for it."

"Sounds like Nelson and Winnie Mandela."

"No Muntaqim, that was dedication for real, brother. She waited for more than two decades for him to get out of that hell hole."

"It was a let down when they got a divorce, Maleek, especially after all of that time."

"A lot of things change and people too, Muntaqim."

Abdul Maleek brought the conversation back in line with the present situation. "I'm in here though, brother, I'm not trying to contemplate on those emotional ties at this time, I still have three years to go so I have to keep it hard."

Abdul Muntaqim nodded his head in approval because he knows that a brother must guard his emotions and keep those feelings under control. Without control of oneself in the penitentiary environment, an inmate can break down emotionally if he doesn't maintain a fight within himself.

When a strong personality emerges within the penitentiary, he can often gain a lot of followers, even to the point of those followers pledging their allegiance to him if that's what their organization dictates.

"You know, Muntaqim," said the Emam. "I've known you since we were on the streets together and even when we were in gangs together that you were always loyal to whatever you were involved with, and you're loyal now."

"We gonna get through this thing together, brother," said Abdul Muntaqim, as he put his hand on the brother's shoulder.

"Speaking of together, Muntaqim, how many brothers are in the community?"

"About seventy five with hundreds of helpers, if we ever needed them."

"That's automatic, everybody seems to be connected to each other in some form or another, if something happens on this end, there's a connection to that group or that group, plus that helps to keep down a lot of static."

"How many brothers in the community have bay'at with the community brother?"

"I think it's sixty...no sixty two because brother Sudan and Bashir offered their allegiance last week, remember on the yard by the bleachers?"

"Yes I remember now, because one of them wasn't washed up properly to handle the Holy Quran."

"I think Johnny Shafeek want to offer his allegiance also."

"Do he have all his lessons and prayers down pat?" asked the Emam.

"All that's in order, brother."

"Time is moving, Muntaqim, when you see Johnny, let him know how the allegiance is given. Explain to him that he'll take his right hand and place it on the Holy Quran, he'll then repeat after me with two or more witnesses present, don't give him the location that we'll meet at until the last minute, this way we can avoid any possible set ups."

"All right, brother, I'm going to let these brothers know about the leadership meeting tonight."

Abdul Muntaqim set out to inform the other brothers in the community about the meeting tonight. The good relationship that the MB's have with some correction officers has enabled Abdul Muntaqim to go into other cellblocks and dorms without any static. H-Block is his first destination.

"C.O., can I see inmate Howard for a minute?" asked Abdul Muntaqim.

"Just for a couple of minutes, I don't want any <u>white shirts</u> sneaking up on me, they already think that I'm too close to the MB's as it is," replied the C.O.

"I appreciate that, Johnson, how's everything been going?"

"You know how it is, Muntaqim, this is just a job for me, I really ain't tryin to make a career out of this, and that's for real."

"Yeah, I know what you mean, it do pay the bills."

"This place is hazardous to a man's health, plus I do not want to be around here when things explode."

"Don't worry about that, Johnson, if something happens we'll make sure that we remember those that treated us right. One thing is for sure, you always treated us with respect, and that counts for a lot up in here."

Abdul Muntaqim finally went to Omar's cell and knocked on the door before looking in. The cellblock is the last area of privacy within the prison that an inmate can go to.

Omar is the assistant Emam; he's thirty-three years old and has been locked up for twelve years. Before coming to Islam, he had killed a couple of dope dealers because of a bad dope deal.

"As-salaam alaikum ,believer, what's going on up this way?" asked Muntaqim.

"Wa-alaikum salaam, my brother, I'm good, all praise is due to Allah."

"I'm passing through to let you know that the Emam wants to have a meeting for all the department heads after the class, if there is any concerns that has to be presented, you can do it then."

"One thing about me, my brother," said Omar, as he brushed off his black velvet fez. "I been doing these meetings for about eight years in here so I know what to expect."

While Muntaqim and Omar discuss the up and coming class, Ronnie Muhammad, a twenty-five year old brother on security walked up. When asked about his mood while doing his time, he always says that he's fearing Allah and exerting himself in the cause of Islam.

"As-salaam alaikum, believers," said Muhammad, walking up on the brothers as close as possible and extending his hands.

"Wa-alaikum salaam, Muhammad,"replied Muntaqim. "I see that you're on the move as usual."

"Just keepin' those in check who need to be checked, you know how I like, I got to stay in the mix for the pleasure of Allah."

"Ain't no mystery, my brother," said Muntaqim, as he put his hand on Muhammad's shoulder. "How's your store going?"

All praise due to, Allah, it's keeping me from doing something wrong around here, like selling some dope or gambling all day long, just to keep some food in my locker box."

"All of this is gonna pass away, I just came by to let Omar know about the meeting tonight, I'll see you brothers later on."

Designated study time has been afforded to the MB's along with the Friday prayer service to conduct their business; classrooms have been provided to them. These gatherings have been vital in counteracting the onslaught of vice, negative ideas, and troublesome inmates, whose purpose is to undermine anything positive that comes into their midst.

Having two to three times a week to come together in order to deal with Islamic concerns, every minute is utilized to its fullest. There are still those who prefer to scale back the number of times that Muslims can meet together on a weekly basis, to thwart a dominant, influencing organization from ever emerging again, and to make sure a leader can't dictate events within the penitentiary as it did at the Lucasville uprising. In that uprising, there was a claim that the MB's had control and that a central figure had emerged as a leader that dictated the events.

Before the Islamic class is to start, the brothers on security are the first to get there. "Brothers, let's shake this room down, everybody knows how it's done; look under the chairs, in the desks, the waste baskets, vents, and everywhere that something can be hidden," commanded Abdul Muntaqim.

"Yeah brother," said Muhammad. "You remember how we found some <u>shanks</u> hid in the ceiling, last time we used this room. That's why I don't like using this room behind the Seven Steppers organization. The ones that's in there now, they ain't nothin' but a bunch of coward racists, hidin' behind some swastikas, lightnin' bolts, and confederate flags. If it was up to me, Muntaqim, we a shut them down, because we in the penitentiary and they can't go and hide nowhere."

"Yeah, Muhammad, we can never let our guard down, that's why I want this room shook down, real good. All it takes is a couple of crooked guards to plant a couple of joints in one of these desks and then come in here and take all of us to the hole."

"That's how they did Billy in H-block last week, everybody knows that he don't mess with that reefer, and all of a sudden some is found in his locker box, somethin' wasn't right with that."

"Muhammad, I want a brother outside the door as usual and make sure to take attendance, because some of these same brothers who be late all the time are the same ones who owe the community money."

The announcement is made over the loud speaker by prison authorities for Islamic class. "Islamic services in room twelve, Islamic services in room twelve."

The classes are open to anyone within the penitentiary, but this is an environment where inmates live in what's considered their own societies.

Being that every type of mentality is under one roof, inmates seek to be around only those they feel comfortable with.

The MB's were given a free hand at one point to come up with new ways to transmit the knowledge of Al-Islam. They were given permission to sell Muslim newspapers to the inmate population, along with some fund raising events.

With the help of the Emam from the outer society, the brothers had come up with an idea that brought three hundred inmates to the meeting in the middle of the week and this went on for a month. This seemed to have taken some prison authorities by surprise.

The Emam from outside the prison had brought in famous films that showed the fights of Muhammad Ali, George Foreman, Joe Frazier, and others. Refreshments were also served with the profits going into the MB's penitentiary account.

This event had become the talk of the penitentiary, some favorable and some not. Inmates would be heard saying, "Hey, ya'll, let's go to the Muslim meeting tonight, they showin' fights." The hallways would become so crowded that guards would be nowhere in sight.

Two to three hundred dollars was made per showing; this new success of making money and getting a large number of inmates to come to a meeting was being watched very closely.

The number of inmates that attended the Muslim functions began to surpass the Catholic, Protestant, and any other religiously based event within the penitentiary. These events were bringing the hardest of the hard inmates out to the Muslim meetings. Inmates, who gave the impression that they were crazy in the eyes of prison authorities, suddenly showed some discipline and came to the meetings to listen to the lectures and watch some fights.

The classrooms were too small to have the events in, so the cafeteria had to be used. The MB's used their own security to secure themselves.

The prison authorities knew that order was the order of the day when the MB's had a large crowd at their events. They used their security to post up around the food, directing inmates to their seats and making sure that everyone had signed cash slips to pay for the refreshments.

This situation was too much like right for some top authorities.

"They're making money, plus they're advancing their way of life to the inmates." It was a dilemma for those prison administrators who knew that the MB's were doing them a service; they kept a lid on potential trouble from inmates who were considered a threat to the overall operations of the penitentiary. Those same inmates were cooperative and respectful when they came to the Muslim inspired functions.

The MB's didn't condemn inmates when they came around telling them that they're wrong about this or that. The Muslims influenced inmates by treating them with respect and making them their equals when they came around. When hardcore inmates experienced this type of treatment, they felt like they belonged to something that wasn't trying to bring them down, so they wanted to become a part of it.

There were a few inmates that stood out because of their physical size and fervor for the new way of life that they had discovered for themselves. They had commanded respect and also some fear before coming to the religion, but had received more respect when they molded their negative ways into something positive.

During the video showings and lectures on Al-Islam, a number of inmates came into the religion. There was this one brother who was large in height and had the look of having shoulder pads under his shirt. He had a reputation outside as well as inside the penitentiary as being on the "watch out" list because of his presence. He usually dictated how events would go on around him wherever he went.

This brother started studying Al-Islam, which had a great impact upon him. The inmates that looked up to him, some of them followed him into the religion.

He quickly learned the Arabic alphabet, started reading the Holy Quran and pushed every program that the Muslims had come up with to promote the religion. When it came to selling Muslim newspapers and oils, he sold so many and received so many donations, that some prison authorities misinterpreted his methods as being extortion. From that situation, the newspaper was no longer allowed to be sold in the open like that again, the videos and food selling was also disbanded.

The MB's had found refuge in their meetings from the harshness of the prison world that called for vigilance whenever someone stepped outside the cell door. Being able to sleep in a cell with the door locked, provided a large measure of security compared to being in a dormitory with ninety to one hundred or more inmates that could snap at anytime.

At the Wednesday's Islamic class, Omar opened up with the Muslim's opening prayer and then went into his lecture.

"All praise is due to Allah, brothers, for giving us another chance to redeem ourselves from that which our own hands have brought us to. Allah says in Chapter two, verse 214, in the Holy Quran, 'Or do you think that ye shall enter the Garden of Bliss, without such trials as came to those who passed before you? They encountered suffering and adversity and were so shaken in spirit that even the messenger and those of faith who were with him, cried, When will come the help of Allah! Ah, verily, the help of Allah is always near!'

Brothers you should always reflect on this verse when you begin to think that you're the only ones that had tests put upon you. One of yours just happened to be the penitentiary. There weren't televisions, radios, hand and tennis ball courts to make the Prophet (pbuh) and his companions tests in life easy, like we have it now. No, some of you think that this is hard; hard is when some of the first brothers in here were trying to establish, Al-Islam. They didn't have a choice of foods to pick from when there was nothing but pork being served on the food lines. There weren't a variety of Islamic materials that we could read from, let alone Holy Qurans brought from all the corners of the globe to help a brother out.

We will always thank those that came before us that strove in this way and made the sacrifices that we don't have to make now. Our predecessors were taken to the hole and beat up while handcuffed by overzealous and illiterate guards, and brothers still come back out saying that they are not deterred from what they believe in.

I'm not going to take up anymore time, because our time for having classes is limited. The Emam wanted me to emphasize to all you brothers, keep up your prayers and remember that it is Allah who will determine when a person shall walk through those front doors to get out. That's one thing that we all look forward to happening for us, to get out, but we must have some patience. I'd like to bring forth the head of security, Abdul Muntaqim, as-salaam alaikum."

"Wa-alaikum salaam."

Abdul Muntaqim came before the brothers; a brother that has a large task, he's a brother that deals with the nitty gritty that goes on within the penitentiary, from negotiating to settling disputes when they arise. He's known throughout the penitentiary as being over the most disciplined group of inmates within the penitentiary.

"As-salaam alaikum, brothers," said Abdul Muntaqim.

"Wa-alaikum salaam."

Abdul Muntaqim opened up with his introduction.

"I bear witness that there is no God but Allah, and Prophet Muhammad in his Messenger. All praise is due to Allah for blessing us to see another day. We all are aware that anything can happen at anytime in here at the spur of the moment. All it takes is one situation to get out of hand in one of these cellblocks or dormitories, and then the domino effect occurs. That's why we say, we thank Allah for another day to strive to improve our situation. Brothers, you all know that I'm head of security, my job is to act as a protector of the community and to be the eyes and ears for the Emam. We'd like to hit some basic concerns this evening.

First of all, brothers should strive to get to class on time. Being punctual is a sign that you are about what you're involved in. I know that some of you brothers growl when you hear about the consequences of being late. You have to pay those fines. Now, if a brother has a legitimate reason for being late, that's understandable. The cut off time is five minutes, after that, the fines go into effect. Any questions pertaining to that issue? Brother Jamil."

"Yes, brother Muntaqim, you know that cigarettes just went up and some of us are not getting any help from home, so I think that some of these fines should be adjusted to the type of income that a brother is making."

"You have a good point, brother, in order for that to be changed, the council would have to agree to it. The majority of the council is here, so I'm sure that your suggestion is definitely being heard.

This is the next point of discussion. You got to stay on guard from those homosexuals around here, we know that the drives of sex and hunger are strong. The hunger, we can all solve that one, but dealing with those homosexuals, we goin' to act strong against that. In Al-Islam, our laws dictate that we don't have intimate relationships with another man. If we drive up on you and we catch you in the act, we're going' to probably have some serious things going on.

Our position is clear on this issue, we're not gonna have any he-she's in our ranks. Now to put this in the language that you new brothers are used to hearing. If we catch you goin' up in one of those boys, it ain't gonna be no talkin'.

We've heard all of the lines that a brother can present when he's somewhere he's not supposed to be. I'm just payin' the boy to wash my clothes, iron my pants or braid my hair. My advice is just don't put yourself in the position that you have to be alone anywhere with them.

Start fasting more and get into your workouts a little stronger. All this is part of the fight; it's a jihad. This internal war is what we have to deal with, and the rest will be easy.

This is the last statement that I'm going to make about this, so that nobody will fall in the same trap. Three months ago when three of the brothers had to go to the hole, for about five months for doing something for the community, because a couple of inmates harassed a young Muslim brother. Well, five months is a long time to be locked down twenty four hours a day, but it don't justify a brother getting weak and then falling in love with one of those boys. That's exactly what happened, a brother fell for another man with Kool-Aid on his cheeks and lips. If it weren't for the Emam telling us to leave it alone, somebody would have hit him in his mouth by now. I'm saying this, the Emam already had spoke on it and there's nothing else to talk about, so we don't want to hear anymore brothers talking about what should have been done.

I'm going to deal with a few more points; the mandatory workouts, receiving suspicious passes, being in the company of those who is selling dope, and allegiance to the community.

The mandatory workouts is just that; designed for all brothers to participate in. We expect all brothers to assemble on the handball court every Saturday morning for the unity workout. The workout consists of running laps around the track in unison; pushups, jumping jacks, the whole nine yards. The workout is finished when every brother puts the boxing gloves on and then spars with each other, all of this is designed to keep us strong in our daily encounters."

"I got a question, can we learn some of that Kung Fu that you and brother Jaleel know about?"

"Yeah, we can do that, as a matter of fact, Jaleel and myself train a few brothers in the gym once in awhile.

Let me caution you brothers on the arts though. In here there's no guns unless someone makes a zip gun. Therefore a man who knows how to use his hands is a threat, not only to the guards but also to the inmates as well, even a coward can stab you in the back, so be cautious.

Another point that we have to cover is suspicious passes. Be careful, it can be a setup, someone could be waiting for you to do some harm.

That's why we always say, have a brother with you no matter where you go. Time after time we see that this is the method used by certain groups, when they're after somebody, they send them a pass."

"Brother Muntaqim, how about if we can't find a brother to be with at the time?"

"Well brother, you have to use some common sense when it comes to some things that you do. If you know that there are a few blind spots that you have to encounter, just be very cautious.

Before I get from up here, I want to say to the brothers, who don't have allegiance with Masjid Jihad, that it's always open to you. With that, I'd like for those without allegiance to excuse themselves from the rest of our community meeting and we thank you for coming, As-salaam alaikum."

"Wa-alaikum salaam."

After the visitors and Muslims without allegiance to the community had left, and before the Amirs conducted their meeting, the financial secretary spoke to the Muslims.

"As-salaam alaikum."

"Wa-alaikum salaam."

"I bear witness that there is no God, but Allah, and Prophet Muhammad (pbuh) is his Messenger. All praise is due to Allah for allowing me to make it through another day so that I can give something back and wipe some of this stain off of my soul. Just briefly, brothers, I have to remind everyone to pay their taxes and some charity along with it. All that we're saying is that a brother should send five dollars a month to a Masjid on the streets. The Masjid can be one that you're affiliated with or you can send something to the Masjid that our servicing, Emam goes to. The brothers that are making some good money off of these oils that we're selling, how about putting a little more money back into the community, that way we all can benefit together. For the sake of time, the Emam had asked me to bring this part of our meeting to a close.

As-salaam alaikum."

"Wa-alaikum salaam."

CHAPTER 4

ONLY FOR US!

The meeting for the department heads often referred to as the Amirs meeting, is what kept the MB's affairs intact. With the leaders of one of the most organized groups of inmates coming together to discuss their community's affairs, the agenda for the fast of the Muslim's month of Ramadan had already been put into motion.

"As-salaam alaikum, brother Emam. We had to take two more brothers off of the Ramadan list, they were caught eating in the café this morning by a couple of guards," reported Abdul Muntaqim.

"Wa-alaikum salaam, brother. Before you took them off the list, did you remind them of my message that I gave to all the brothers before the fast had started?"

"Yes, brother, I definitely did, I told them that a Muslim conceals the faults of his brother, but when a brother brings his faults in the open for everyone to see without regard for the impact that it'll have on the community of brothers. He can start eating from his locker box, day and night. Also, he doesn't have to worry about coming down to break his fast with the rest of us in the evening."

"All praise is due to Allah, Muntaqim, we got to keep it tight, otherwise things will fall apart."

"You're right, brother."

"Anything else that I should know about?"

"Yeah, brother Emam, there's this new brother that was transferred from another penitentiary. He got on the list to fast without going through us. I informed him that everything we do around here is organized and not done in a haphazard way. He seems to be evasive about where he came from, so I'm going to check with some sources in the records office to see where he came from; plus, I'll talk to him again tonight when we go to break our fast."

"That's a good move, brother, from what you told me about him, he knows a little something about the religion."

"Yeah, he's familiar with the stipulations concerning the fast, but understanding them might be a different story."

"I see its about time for the afternoon prayer, I'll see you and the rest of the brothers tonight."

During the fast, the Muslims cook and set up their own meals and then serve themselves. This is one occasion that no one outside of the Islamic community interferes with; the majority of times, the meals are good; consisting of fish, chicken, foods made from soy, fruit, vegetables, and plenty to drink. Nothing is thrown away." Prison employees had a habit of throwing away large quantities of food that was leftover from meals served to the inmates earlier in the day.

When Ramadan came around, the big test emerged. It was so much food unlike any other time of the year those brothers had access to, that the temptation to over indulge was ever present. It was like a person receiving a large sum of money after being broke for a long period of time. Some of that money is going to be squandered, unless some principles of saving are introduced.

After standing in line all year behind hundreds of inmates three times a day with food being rationed out, the fast of Ramadan became a blessing in more ways than one. There were no long lines to stand in when it came time to eat no competition with other inmates for a seat while eating, no pork to smell and no guards standing around asking anyone to leave the cafeteria.

On the personal side, the fast of Ramadan presented an opportunity for those brothers with a nagging conscience of some past events, to engage in every aspect of the fast that presented some type of forgiveness for their deeds.

As more inmates began to learn about Al-Islam, they knew that there was something magic about the fast. Brothers would be transformed into more humble individuals, there would be less talk and less participation in events that they would do throughout the year.

The fast especially interested those without any type of significant system in their life. When inmates saw changes in those who fasted in a short thirty day period, they figured that it had to be due to the knowledge that they were feeding upon that produced that change ,so every year the list to sign up to participate in the fast became larger and larger.

"You brothers watch out how much food that you take out of this cafeteria," said the Emam. "The warden had already agreed with us on how much food can be taken back in our bags for our morning meal, so don't try to take anything extra out."

"Emam, this is just what I have to talk to the new brother about," said Muntaqim. "He insists on trying to do things his own way, he's taking food out of the cafeteria and already been caught twice, but check this out, he only been working in the kitchen for three days."

"Go and talk to him, Muntaqim. See if you can appeal to him to slow down."

"I'll approach him again because we're going to have to straighten this out, it's bringing too much heat on our community."

As the brothers started to assemble in the cafeteria to break their fast with something to drink and then to perform their prayers, Abdul Muntaqim and his assistant approached brother Razzaq.

"We'd like to talk to you brother," the head of security had said. Jumping up from his seat, the new brother started yelling.

"Ahhh, they comin' at me!"

"What's wrong with you?" Abdul Muntaqim stated calmly. "All that yellin' ain't necessary, you crazy or something, all we want to do is talk to you."

A correction officer on patrol just happened to be passing by the cafeteria, heard the noise then he came in. "You, you, and you, get up against the wall!" he shouted, while calling for some backup. "I got a light disturbance in the cafeteria, send a couple of officers."

"See what you done," growled Muntaqim. "You disrupted our fast."

"What's the problem here, what's the yelling all about?" asked the correction officer, while pulling out his handcuffs and cautiously looking around at all the brothers starting to stand up from the tables that they were eating at.

"They pulled up on me, I feel threatened," yelled the inmate, who appeared to be on some type of medication.

"I'm going to have to take you three to the hole until we get this situation straightened out," commanded the correction officer.

"Don't you brothers worry, we're going to take care of you while you're in the hole," shouted Omar, with the other brothers nodding their heads in agreement. "That includes you too, brother."

Two days later, the Emam, his assistants, and four other department heads were summoned to the sergeant's office. On the way to the office, the Emam spoke on some of the strategy that they'll use when questioned.

"When we get into this guy's office, brother Omar will do the talking. The rest of us will just listen because I have no idea what this clown wants," said the Emam. "This way I can evaluate what is going on.

"Okay brother," replied Omar. "This guy just got promoted to a higher job and he's still wearing that old sergeant's uniform."

"Oh yeah," said Emam Maleek.

"It was something about a racial balance promotion, the order came from Columbus, so I know that this guy is going to be looking to score some points for real."

"You know, Omar, said the Emam. "I been wondering why he been coming after everything black around here. When he got promoted, the higher ups knew exactly what they were doing. They put a guy like that in charge of a hostile environment like this, and the first thing he does is try and show that he's not biased in his job and then it's overkill."

"Yeah, he's been locking up a lot of brothers lately and looks like he's not letting up," said Omar.

"If he asks any questions pertaining to organization, let me handle it," replied the Emam. "Because no telling what this is all about."

"Yes, brother." Inside the office of the newly appointed deputy warden who was still wearing his old uniform, he was ready to have his first conversation about a topic that he suspected, but had never tried to verify about the Muslim leadership.

"I called you guys in my office because we seem to have a problem here," the deputy warden said. "I need some information."

"What seems to be the problem?" asked Omar, establishing the face that he's the spokesman for the brothers, from this reply, the deputy warden keyed in on whom he suspected was the leader. From his experience when dealing with the prison's security for so long, those inmates who are often the leaders are often the ones to speak first.

"This is the problem," said the deputy warden. "I have three of you Muslims in the hole and one of them will not be coming back out because of what he told us about you brothers. As a matter of fact, we're sending him to another penitentiary. As for the other two, I'm going to keep them in there for about a week until my investigation is complete."

All six of the brothers just nodded their heads, no emotions were shown, they just waited to see what was next.

"My question is this," asked the deputy warden. "Who is the top Amir supposed to be and what's this about some of you being sent on missions based on somebody giving you some orders?"

Emam Maleek suddenly spoke up. "I don't know what someone told you, Deputy Warden, but we don't have anybody that we refer to as Amirs and as far as somebody being sent on missions, I don't know why that new inmate would tell you something like that. We're not trying to be a leader over anyone; we're in here just trying to complete our time so that we can get back to our families, there's a few fights now and then and that's about all, you've seen that."

The deputy warden stared in Maleek's eyes looking for a twitch or a sign of deception which he had developed a keen eye for from dealing with hundreds of inmates over the years.

"You guys can go for now, I'm going to be watching all of you, my new job includes being the director of institutional programs, so you'll be seeing me more often."

As the brothers began to move out, the deputy warden said one more thing. "Oh, I forgot to remind you inmates one more thing, that other Muslim won't be coming back out here again, because we know that it didn't sit well with you guys about him informing us what you are all about."

Once again the brothers remained quiet until they left from the warden's office.

"Remember this, brothers," said the Emam. "The Prophet had said in the book of war, that war is a strategy, and I'm saying this, if you brothers don't realize that we're in a war, you had better analyze your situation again."

"Man, that snitch went and told about some of our operations," said an angry Omar. "Ain't nobody never asked us about something like that, after all these years."

"Make sure that those brothers are well taken care of, Omar, that's our family; they hurt and we hurt."

That was the beginning of a scrutiny that was well beyond what the MB's were ever used to. The threat of strong leaders with the power to command other inmates was the type of threat that prison officials knew can undermine the security of the penitentiary. To have black inmates too powerful seemed to be somewhat of a bigger threat, mainly because of the sheer numbers that they had, and the rawness of angry inmates that can emerge at any given time. So it was always best to make sure that no strong organization got control over the thinking of a majority of inmates in the eyes of the prison administrators.

In the Amirs meeting after the regular Islamic class was over, the Emam and the other department heads met to discuss community business. The Emam began the meeting with a request.

"With the name of Allah, most gracious, most merciful. Secretary Jihad, I want you to write a letter to a few of the Islamic organizations in the United States as well as abroad; and let them know that when they send free Holy Qurans to just any inmate without knowing if they are a Muslim or not, they should contact the Muslim community within the prison first. Our reasoning is this,'we're running into problems with those who receive the Quran's, in that they don't understand what they have and this is what I mean.

We do not take our Holy Quran's into the bathrooms, as we have some of those who received the Holy Quran from your organization doing now. In the dormitories, where bathrooms are in a separate section from the sleeping area, we have found a few inmates reading the Holy Quran while sitting on the toilet. This is the way that inmates treat the Bible. The Muslims in here don't tolerate that with the Holy Quran. We feel that people have to be trained and should be instructed about some things before engaging in them.

With Al-Islam spreading like a wildfire within these prisons in the United States, we feel that there should be a more conscientious effort on the part of gracious donors such as yourself, to the sensitivities of the Muslims, when we see our Holy Quran mishandled by those who have no knowledge of what they have. It's different out there, where people, who are not Muslims, may purchase a Holy Quran and taken them behind closed doors, you can't see how they're treating them. In the penitentiary, everything is in the open for everyone to see, we cannot tolerate those going to the bathroom or laying the Holy Quran down by their feet.

We propose that something in the way of instructions be included with any Holy Quran that you send. Here's an example:

1. The Holy Quran should not be taken into the bathroom.

2. It should be respected at all times and pages not torn out.

3. It should not be mixed up with pronographic magazines.

4. Ask Muslims that may be in your midst to help you understand the Holy Quran.

5. Keep it on the highest shelf that may be in your midst.

We appreciate your help in this matter, may Allah bless you for your good works.

As-salaam alaikum,

Emam Maleek and the members of Masjid Jihad. I want that letter duplicated brother secretary, and the first letter sent out tomorrow."

"How do you want this done, through our own account or use our own people?"

"Our own people, because that new deputy warden might try to start monitoring our mail."

"I wouldn't put it past him, brother Emam."

"Don't forget to let the brother know that we appreciate this favor because some things we just don't want to go through the regular mail."

"Pertaining to those Holy Quran's, brother Emam, we've been approaching those inmates that we know have them," said the head of security. "And we've been instructing them on how to handle the book properly. Those who think that they can do what they want to with the Quran, we've been persuading them that it's in their best interest to listen to us, especially when it comes to a book that we cherish and there will be no compromise about it."

"Stay on top of that, Muntaqim, because that's all we got. Brother Omar, I think that you had something to say also."

"As-salaam alaikum, brothers."

"Wa-alaikum salaam."

"We have a new brother that became a Muslim down south at the maximum security prison and he just arrived here yesterday. He's been down for five years now and his security status has dropped because of good behavior. Well, this is the problem; before he came into the penitentiary, he caught a murder case when he robbed a man coming out of a store, the guy that he killed, well, his son is in the same block as the Emam and myself. We got word of who he was when we found out that he was trying to buy a shank, so we know what that means."

"Excuse me, Omar, let me say this," interrupted the Emam. "Ray is bent on revenge. The brother whose name is Aquil is serving out his time and been judged by the outside courts, but now, we all know that there's the law of the penitentiary; the law of revenge and that's where we come in at, because the brother is a Muslim now.

We're told in the sayings of the Prophet (pbuh) that we should guard a brother's blood, honor, and wealth. Higher still though, when somebody comes into the religion with sincerity and strives to fulfill their obligations to Allah, he forgives them for their past bad deeds.

This is a very emotional issue that we're dealing with because Ray doesn't want to hear no talking. His father been killed and the one who killed him is now a Muslim, and no one is going to harm any Muslims around here.

Abdul Muntaqim, I want you to go to Ray one more time and keep him off balance for awhile. While you're doing that, we're going to see if we can get Aquil transferred to another penitentiary. If we don't, there's going to be some blood spilt around here somewhere. This is why I believe that it's best to get this brother out of here, so that we can avoid any future trouble.

I can understand how Ray must feel. Imagine someone killing one of our fathers and then they're brought in here with us. So this is my decision, I want this moved on just as soon as this meeting is over."

"It's done." replied Abdul Muntaqim.

"It's time to move on to other issues, brother Muntaqim, what do you have for us in the way of security?"

"As-salaam alaikum, brothers."

"Wa-alaikum salaam."

"All praise is due to Allah, in the time of peace we have to stay ready for war, never again will we ever let anybody get the upper hand over us. No matter how many prayers we make a day, we should never forget where we're at and the type of mentalities that we're forced to deal with everyday. That was the key word my brothers, forced to deal with. We can't go and hide in a cave somewhere and put our faces under the covers, At this point, we have fifteen sukeenuuns, eighteen pipes, and ten hoods for our use when needed."

"Is everything spread around like we discussed?" asked the Emam.

"Yes, it is brother. As far as the brothers in the hole are concerned, we're making sure that all of them have their Holy Qurans, envelopes, and writing paper. This is why I made a request last week from the finance department for more packs of cigarettes, so that we can pay the porters to get our goods back to our brothers.

Pertaining to our codes, no one knows certain brothers names except the Emam, the first Amir, and myself. That's only for us, this is for the protection of our community and this leadership while we're in this prison. I have to keep emphasizing to you brothers over and over again, that we're not on the streets. It may seem that we take a hard line on some issues, but we have to deal with everything that pops up and I'm not leaving anything to chance. My policy is this; all threats are going to be dealt with immediately and not later."

"I have a question," said the head of the finance department, brother Luqman. "I think that the Amirs should be more informed about what's going on pertaining to some security matters because that's something that affects everyone in here. I realize that we can't be informed about everything that goes on within the security department, but at least about more than what we have been getting."

"This is for sure, brother Luqman," replied Abdul Muntaqim. "If something major happens or comes up, I always alert the whole community. Everything is not meant for everyone. The more a brother knows around here the more he's responsible for, I can live with that. I accept that fact that something's done around here can't be handled by everybody, this is why brothers like the Emam, Omar, and myself, who have been together doing this for the past few years, are cautious about the type of information that we let out into the community, because we never know who is who, until we work with them for awhile. Look at that situation where that young brother in the other community was put out after coming to know all that he came to know about certain brothers. Now, for him to be killed on the yard like that was a bold move. I'd rather be more cautious about giving too much information out than to have something like that occur based on a brother knowing something about how we operate, then leaving the religion and telling about everything that occurred."

"Let's move on," said the Emam.

"I'm developing new codes for the community as our membership continues to grow because we've seen in the past, that everyone that comes among us does not have allegiance to the community, so everyone stay watchful," said Abdul Muntaqim, as he finished up his address to the community.

"All praise is due to Allah," continued Emam Maleek. "It's always good to know that security is always near. Let's move on to an important aspect that touches all of us and that's education.

Even though he can get long winded at times, we know that he has a lot to say, the head of the education department, brother Jaleel."

"As-salaam alaikum, brothers," said Jaleel.

"Wa-alaikum salaam."

"With the name of Allah, most gracious, most merciful. The education department is running smooth, every new member is given what I call a packet. All the brothers who don't have a Holy Quran are given one and shown how to handle it. They are then directed to the classes on Wednesday, the beginning and advanced Arabic class is on Saturday, and Sunday is orientation day. Oh yeah, and on Friday is our congregational prayer services.

As outlined in our constitution, all brothers are required to know the five pillars of Al-Islam, the six cardinal articles of faith, the six points, and the six duties that a Muslim owes to his brother. He has to know these before he can hold any major positions within the community.

Here's an updated copy of that which I just described.

FIVE PILLARS OF FAITH

1. Declaration of Faith - There is no God but, Allah, and Muhammad is his Messenger.

2. Prayers - Five times a day.

3. Charity - Two and one half- percent of one's total gross earnings.

4. Fasting - During the month of Ramadan.

5. Pilgrimage - Journey to the Holy City of Mecca, at least once in ones lifetime.

SIX CARDINAL ARTICLES OF FAITH

1. Belief in the oneness of Allah.

2. Belief in the Angels.

3. Belief in the Prophets.

4. Belief in the Holy Books.

5. Belief in the day of Resurrection and Judgment.

6. Belief in Predestination.

SIX POINTS

1. Faith.

2. Prayer.

3. Intentions.

4. Knowledge and remembrance of Allah.

5. Want for your brother what you want for yourself.

6. Transmitting knowledge, propagation.

SIX DUTIES A MUSLIM OWES TO HIS BROTHER

1. To give advice when he's asked for it.

2. To accept his invitations.

3. To pray for him when he sneezes.

4. To visit him when he's sick.

5. To respond to his greetings.

6. To attend his funeral.

"Each brother should know these by heart and once a brother does that, we then go into the depth of them. From there everyone is required to read up on the life of the Prophet Muhammad (pbuh), the traditional schools of thought, and the history of the development of Al-Islam in North America and the movements that followed. We start with the history of Noble Drew Ali, Fard Muhammad and the Nation of Islam and then we teach about some of the major leaders that emerged form the movements they started. The brothers are taught at the beginning of class that it's better to know a little about something, than to be ignorant of it.

After the completion of orientation class, each brother is given a certificate, once they demonstrate a knowledge on how to perform their prayers."

"Sounds like a good education curriculum, brother Jaleel," said the Emam. "All praise is due to Allah. This concludes our department heads meeting. Let's close out with the name of Allah, most gracious, most merciful."

CHAPTER 5

WARNINGS, WAR TALK, OPERATIONS

"Would you listen to and obey your ruler at the time when you are tired, and that you would not fight against the ruler or disobey him, and would you stand firm for the truth, or say the truth wherever you might be, and in the way of Allah, you would not be afraid of the blame from the blamers?" Sahih Bukhari Vol. 9, Chapter 43.

"Brother Emam, those same guys are at it again, they're trying to undermine, Al-Islam!" said Abdul Muntaqim. "I'm going to check 'em hard this time!"

"Just hold up, brother," said Emam Maleek. "Who are you talking about this time?"

"A couple of those guys who call themselves, Black Hebrews, they're going around talking about Al-Islam is supposed to fall in five years."

"Man, we just got finished warning those guys about coming behind everything we do, trying to undermine our teaching efforts," replied the Emam. "What they're trying to do is tear somebody else down in order to gain some members for their ranks."

"That was just last week, brother Emam, we told them just last week to stop approaching inmates that we're trying to teach about Al-Islam, that this is the wrong way to go."

"I tell you what, brother Muntaqim, take a few brothers with you and give them this message directly from me. That if they don't stop trying to undermine our way of life, it's going to be some blood."

Among some groups of inmates, there are those who become jealous because they think that the Muslims receive special treatment, from Ramadan, the Islamic classes, to the right of the brothers to wear their headgear and fezzes when and where they want to, caused some inmates to look for anything that they can to try to undermine the religion.

If it wasn't for the strength and organization that the MB's displayed, the inner rage of some groups would turn into an attack, but, physical attacks on Muslims were very rare, mainly because of the repercussions that such an attack would bring on the attacker.

There were some members of the Black Hebrews who had a tendency of causing some mischief often times unknowingly. In their attempts to teach black inmates about their history, they would get to the period about Al-Islam, and try to make it sound like it was the religion that put Africans into bondage. This was an underhanded attempt to thwart the positive effect, that Al-Islam was having on the black inmate population.

Great contributions to civilization from Africans who were Muslims were never mentioned, but were covered up intentionally. To the MB's, this became another way to slander Al-Islam. In a closed environment such as the penitentiary, where there's honor in a persons ideology, whether it's good or bad, the rule is that you don't go around slandering that ideology, the freedom to go around and say what you want doesn't play out too well in here.

"Brother Muntaqim," asked the Emam. "How many times have we tried to come to an understanding with these brothers?"

"Well, let's see. There was the time when they were going around the penitentiary with some papers in their hands, saying that we worshiped a black stone in Mecca."

The Emam nodded his head. "The second time was when they were using the turmoil that was in the countries of Egypt, Syria, Iraq, and Iran as being a sign that Islam was going to fall in five years."

"Right, I remember that, it seemed like they were going into a rage, trying their best to discredit anything associated with the religion.

You know, Muntaqim, they fail to realize that the Muslims have a foothold in the penitentiary among black inmates for decades and now you're starting to see white and Spanish Muslims come in the ranks."

"What do you want me to do, brother Emam?"

"Wait a minute, there was one last situation that really made my mind up about them, remember when a couple of 'em was mishandling the Holy Quran?"

"Yeah, brother, that organization from Pakistan and South Africa sent those Quran's to them."

"They were talking about they were looking for some flaws in the book. That was really the last straw, brother Muntaqim, tell them that there will be no more warnings once you deliver this one. If they don't stop going around trying to undermine Al-Islam, and mishandling our Holy Quran, were coming strapped with our swords out, and it's going to be some blood."

"I'm gonna move on that right now, brother."

OPERATION RESPONSE

One nineteen year old, black inmate, asked an older white inmate about his tattoos on a hot summer day in the prison's gym.

"Hey man, what do those lightning bolts on your neck mean?"

"It means that I killed a nigger," said the professed Nazi.

"Oh yeah, well kill this!" the young inmate yelled with anger, as he threw the older prisoner's whole body into a glass display window that was filled with trophies, causing his head to hit the glass first and splitting open, blood everywhere.

Inside the ranks of the white supremacy group who call themselves the Aryan Brotherhood (AB), talk of revenge spread throughout the penitentiary.

"You hear what happened to our brother Danny in the gym? Some nigger threw his head into a glass window yesterday. They took him to an outside hospital and stitchin' his head up now."

"We didn't hear anything on his condition yet," said one of the members to the other four on the yard watching an inmate baseball game.

"Anybody know who done it?" asked the leader.

"All the information we got was that some bald headed, short nigger with dark skin done it."

"Since we can't pinpoint who done it, Terry, put the word out that we're goin' to kill a nigger tomorrow."

Within the closed walls of the penitentiary, rumors or a word of an event spreads fast. With no barriers to thwart the flow of information, the threat had reached the ears of everyone.

In the cafeteria, Abdul Maleek, brother Omar, and a couple of other brothers were eating their lunch when Abdul Muntaqim pulled up.

"As-salaam alaikum, believers."

"Wa-alaikum salaam, brother, what's up?" replied the Emam.

"I just got word that the AB is talkin' about in their words, they gonna kill a nigger, based on that situation that happened in the gym yesterday."

"I can understand that they want to get back, but talking about killing somebody without specifying who they're talking about, now that's a different story," replied the Emam.

"That's a threat to us too, brother Emam," said brother Omar. "Any coward can easily pick up a shank and stab a brother in the back."

"Those AB boys have been getting pretty bold lately, Maleek," said Abdul Muntaqim. "It seems like the more that they go unchallenged, the bolder they get."

"They may get away with a lot of that bullshit on the streets, but one thing is for sure, brothers," said Abdul Maleek. "We will never let them get the upper hand on us in here because we will shut them down with the quickness.

What we need though is a response. These cowards just can't go around putting out threats to just anybody. Brothers, we're gonna put into effect "Operation Response." Our whole purpose will be to make sure that all those racist cowards know who the MB's are. Also, the fact has to be known, that if anything, no matter how small it is, is done to hurt any Muslim within this penitentiary or in this state by anybody associated with us, we're going to spill some blood in here."

"What you want me to do, brother Emam? Name it and it's done." said the head of security.

"Go and tell all the brothers in the community to meet on the yard at five o'clock. I want everybody in their black sweat suits, black boots, and headgear, because we're getting ready to send a message."

"Any weapons, brother Emam?"

"Just you, Muntaqim, you're the only one that I want to carry a sukeenuun because you're going to watch my back."

"That's always been and always will be, brother."

"Brother Omar, I want you to let the other community know what we're about to do, but only a couple of minutes before we go. This way they can't say that we didn't honor the treaty that we had agreed to concerning notification. Let's go get prepared, and bring some of that cake with you, we can eat some of that on the way to the cellblock."

At five o'clock all the brothers in Masjid Jihad met on the yard with no hesitation, everybody dressed in black sweat suits and boots.

"Abdul Muntaqim, get the brothers in two rows and then I want you and the first Amir standing with me before the brothers."

As the MB's began to assemble on the yard, allies began to come from everywhere and ask, "Ya'll need some help? What ya'll goin' to do?" The reply was always, "We takin' care of this one ourselves."

"You see those cameras focusing in on us, brother Emam," said an observant security member. "The guards will probably be out here in a minute."

"Yeah, I see 'em brother. I got something for that though," said the Emam.

Standing before sixty brothers, all with allegiance to the community, the Emam spoke in the open yard next to the basketball court. It was now time to lay down instructions that was intended to thwart any physical harm coming to the MB's, otherwise, "Operation Response," would have to be implemented.

"As-salaam alaikum."

"Wa-alaikum salaam."

"With the name of Allah, most gracious, most merciful. All praise due to Allah, my brothers, we thank Allah for giving us another day to redeem ourselves from that which our own hands have brought forth. I called this operation in response to a threat made by some racist cowards, which we don't bar none. All of us heard about the situation that happened in the gym yesterday. When it comes to feuds, we have a policy that we don't get involved unless it's going to affect us in some kind of way.

I know a few of you are asking, well, what do this have to do with us, that we have to come out like this. Well, the AB made some broad threats in reference to killing any black inmate. This is one move that they would be making a big mistake on, let alone saying something out of their mouth like that. With all the pinned up frustration that black inmates have in here, combined with the large numbers that they consist of, they really don't want to go that route.

Our situation is limited on this operation to protecting the brothers of our community. Everyone knows how I operate when it comes to protecting the brothers of our community, and you also know that I stand up to the decisions that I do make.

All praise is due to Allah, the special relationship that we have developed over the years with each other as Muslims, and then for you brothers to give your allegiance to this office, brings us to the point that you have to be called upon to deal with situations such as this.

This is our plan; first of all, if any guards come out here, we'll break up in groups of five, we'll then reassemble in the hallway in two columns. The first Amir will be out front, myself in the middle, and the rest of security will bring up the rear. We'll proceed to walk from one end of the hall to another, no talking, just business. From the hallway, we'll go into the gym, Brother Omar will take one column past the weight pile and brother Muhammad will take the other column past the boxing area, we'll meet up by the basketball court and then walk out the door together.

The head of security has just informed me that a group of AB members, along with their leaders is watching a baseball game. Once we get over there, we'll merge our two columns into a single file and walk past the AB. The single line should extend well beyond the three bleachers that the AB occupies. We'll then stop right in front of them, this way they can get a good look at every brother and come to know that these brothers with the black headgear on their heads are not to be messed with. When I give the signal, which the head of security will recognize, we're going to occupy every exit that leads to the inside of this penitentiary. I want ten brothers on each of those five exits, nothing is coming in and nothing is going out unless it's some of our allies or other MB's.

As I said earlier, our message is that no one will touch anyone in these ranks, and that if something drastic did happen to a brother by any of those cowards in the AB, my order is that the leader, the next one in charge, and the recruiter are to be taken out in one of those body bags."

After Operation Response was put into effect, there was no retaliation from the AB, they grumbled a little bit, but that was not going to be the last time that they raised their heads.

OPERATION COUNTERACT

MB's only intervened into a situation that they felt would bring them in anyway. The thinking was, if brought into a conflict; they would have to take control of it themselves, instead of some other group dictating the circumstances.

Avoidance was a non-issue when it came to something major happening within the penitentiary. The saying, "Nowhere to run to and nowhere to hide," was definitely a true slogan.

In order not to be drawn into a larger conflict that would have some dire consequences to it, "Operation Counteract," was devised. There was something about the racist group, the AB, that kept them looking for some type of physical confrontation on a constant basis; be it in the form of sending their members on hits, or just fighting someone to keep up an image of being strong.

So-called Nazi's, skinheads, and some want to be Ku Klux Klansmen, made up the membership of the AB, along with general population inmates, who felt that they wanted to become a part of something.

With no place to hide, no explosives, no guns, some so-called racists in the penitentiary just join these groups because they can't find anything else to do. A lot of times when prisoners come into the penitentiary and come into contact with raw inmates that came from the inner city for the first time, they are usually persuaded to join the AB for protection.

There would rarely be any racial confrontations between black and white groups; mainly because of the large groups of inmates that would get involved. When a racial conflict did occur, it took a lot for the black inmates to stop. It would be like something would snap and there would be no turning back until the whole penitentiary would be shut down and everyone would be locked up.

The AB would wear their tattoos consisting of the swastika, the confederate flag, pictures of Adolph Hitler which some would salute every morning, and lightning bolts. One tattoo had almost started a riot one day. It was a picture of a hooded Klansman with a rope and a black man next to him. Some gang members called the OG's, had confronted the one who had the tattoo and the rest of his crew on the prison yard, they had advised him to either cover it up or get ready for war.

To the Muslims, it was a situation that as long as the AB didn't come in their face with their policies or interfering with what they were doing, there wouldn't be any problem. The Muslims knew that there had to be a great deal of toleration because of the various groups that existed around the prison. After all, this was the penitentiary where everything imaginable was lumped together, and some inmates understanding about some things would take a long time to happen. The best thing the MB's could do in some situations was at least to just hate a thing in their heart and then keep moving, otherwise, they would be in conflict everyday.

The AB started to behave more aggressively when their numbers began to increase and reports from the MB's efforts of gathering information on them, showed that the AB was starting to make more weapons. The MB's had infiltrated the AB with the help of some white inmates who were friends of a couple of the brothers, this is what helped the brothers know what was going on.

Demands by the AB such as not wanting to be in the same cell as black inmates kept the tension high among other things. Some of them said that their religion dictated that they don't intermingle with blacks, which was also referred to as mud people. Even though black inmates preferred to cell with other black inmates, it really wasn't an issue that they were willing to go to the hole for. The AB members were so adamant about the cell integration policy, that it was one of their demands in the prison riot at Lucasville, Ohio in 1993.

The AB began to up the ante. They were beginning to move around in larger groups having little skirmishes here and there, and getting bolder. They had gotten so bold, that they had sent four older members, middle twenties to early thirties, to jump on a nineteen year old black inmate, who was from the largest city within the state, and therefore had what's called the most homies in the penitentiary with him. There was getting ready to be a free for all as far as a battle was concerned, and once that started, no one would be able to escape the domino effect. The force of bottled up frustration, tension, humiliation, and oppression, all comes out with the swiftness, and the results are death and injury until inmates are just tired, or until some tanks and swat team members arrive to squash the rebellion.

At first the authorities wouldn't do anything about the mission that the four AB members were sent on. They looked at it as business as usual, no one was killed so it was left alone, but it wasn't business as usual to some inmates who kept an eye on the AB. This was an escalation of aggression that some inmates knew what to do about and some didn't.

"Man, those hunkies jumped on our homie. We got to do somethin' about this!" said a loose group of about five, young black inmates, who seemed to be oblivious to the time that they must serve as prisoners, as they were swept up in the tide of the emotion at the moment.

Emam Abdul Maleek just happened to come past the commotion, already tuned in to what happened the day before. "What's the matter, young brothers?"

"Man, Maleek, those cowards jumped on our homie, we gonna deal with 'em."

A natural instinct caused the Emam to take charge of the loose band of inmates, nothing planned, it just happened.

"Let's go see if they're in the gym," said Abdul Maleek, while actually trying to put a lid on this explosive situation by taking charge of it. There were quite a few young brothers like these five within the ranks of the Muslim communities in the penitentiary who still had connections to the organizations, called the Bloods, Folks, Crips, and Original Gangsters. They were constantly making transitions to Al-Islam, and reaching back to get others. This was one reason why there were cousins, brothers, nephews, or somebody's uncle, connected to some type of group somewhere, and what affected a few people had an effect on others.

Abdul Maleek and the five hardened young inmates walked into the gym, towards the weight room. The head of the AB, the one who gave the order and three other members were just about to lift some weights.

"There goes some of 'em now!" shouted out one of the young inmates, as Abdul Maleek and the others, walked towards them.

"What the hell ya'll do some shit like that for," one of the inmates yelled, while drawing attention from the other weight lifters.

"What's wrong with everybody?" replied the leaders of the AB. "One guy gets roughed up a little bit and everybody get all out of shape about it."

"We should get with you bitches, right now!" said an inmate, not more than twenty-one years old.

"No!" said Abdul Maleek. "This is neither the time or the place. We're going to do this right. What we're going to do is get with those who actually jumped on your homie. I'm gonna come up with something, let's get out of here."

Abdul Maleek went back to the block, knowing that things had simmered down for a moment. His next appointment was with the head of security to discuss the current potential blow up.

"What's up Johnson?" Abdul Maleek said to the young correction officer, as he came to see Abdul Muntaqim.

"How you doin' Maleek? What are you going to do about that racial hit because I want to be in the know so that I can get out of the way? I will call off from work with the quickness."

"You been here, how long Johnson? About a year and a half now, right?"

"It's going on two years, Maleek."

"Since you been here, when can you recall a situation that came close to this, that didn't have a response to it?"

"Good point, Maleek."

"In actuality, Johnson, that young boy shouldn't have tried to beat those guys out of that money. I mean it was stupid to use some fake money, when they were looking for cash. It still didn't take four of them to jump on him. That guy that's in charge of them should have known that anything that deals with black and white is going to touch a lot of nerves and that includes guards as well as inmates."

"That's the penitentiary law for real, Maleek."

"I got an idea on how to squash all of this without any bloodshed, Johnson. If I don't, the Muslims will be brought in it by the domino effect."

"I hear you, Maleek, because yawl the ones that have to live here, so take care of your business. You want some of this homemade apple pie that my wife made for me?"

"You know it, anytime you got some of that homemade food in here, set it out, because it's been eight years since I was at one of those tables in the house sitting back, and just eating some hot home-cooked food."

"I understand, Maleek."

"Thanks for the pie, Johnson. I got to go see Abdul Muntaqim for a minute."

"Take care, Maleek, it's almost time for me to go home, I'll see you tomorrow."

"Peace to you, brother."

Abdul Maleek walked over to Abdul Muntaqim's cell, knocking on the door and giving the greetings before looking in.

"As-salaam alaika, believer, come on out of that cell for a moment and bring some of those pastries that Fareeda sent you in that food box yesterday."

"Wa-alaika salaam, Maleek. I'm just watching the three o'clock news, that's all."

"Let me see you for a moment, brother."

"Do you still want one of those Danish rolls, brother?"

"No thanks, brother, I just had some apple pie, did you get any bean pie in?"

"That was the first thing I ate, brother, that pie had me thinking that I was back on the streets eating in a Muslim restaurant somewhere."

"When is the next time that Fareeda is going to bring your son, Tareek, up to see you?"

"They're coming in a couple of weeks. Tareek just turned nine last month so he's growing up fast."

"They all are, Muntaqim, we're in our thirties; we came in here in our middle twenties, so time have really moved on."

Both of the brothers just paused for a few seconds, catching themselves, not wanting to enter a world that was miles away, and into a future that was not certain.

"What do you want to get with me about, Maleek?"

"We're going to have to take charge of this potential conflict. That way we can control it without bringing us to the point that we wouldn't possibly like. By ourselves, we never seem to have a problem with the AB because they know not to come this way, plus we don't be in those circles that brings that type of element."

"What's the plan, brother?"

"Go to every black group within the penitentiary; the Bloods, Crips, Folks, Original Gangsters, and Black Hebrews. Let them know that we're going to have to form an alliance. Tell them that we're going to have to meet, the purpose of the meeting will be to come up with plans to make sure the AB will not be able to raise their hands against any one associated with us without paying a high price, and that price will be blood.

"Name the day and time, Maleek."

"Tell 'em Friday, at six o'clock, that way we got two days to prepare and get the word out, plus, everybody will be out of school and off work so it shouldn't be any problem getting there."

"Plus, brother Emam, all of the organizations have been waiting to unite against these racists for quite some time now. There just haven't been anyone strong enough to bring them under one umbrella, but here we are."

"All these young brothers need, brother Muntaqim, is some guidance and being that we're close up on them, we can show them the reality of what this is all about."

"Al-Islam, brother."

"Look at young, Abdul Shaheed, look at how much influence he still has with the Gangster Disciples, his old way of life, they still respect him as a Muslim. The brother must have had some rank among them, because he can still get them together based off of his word."

"Yeah, he was raw wasn't he?" said the head of security.

"I can bear witness to this fact though, when he got a bite of these teachings, all of that rawness turned into fineness, especially when he read about the book of war.

Since I'm out moving around, Muntaqim, I'll let the rest of security know what's going on, As-salaam alaika."

"Wa-alaika salaam, brother."

Friday had come around, the Muslims had come back from Jumma services, ate dinner, and were preparing to put "Operation Counteract" into effect. Those in the penitentiary, who were supposed to be informed about the meeting, were ready also.

The inmates weren't the only ones who were ready; so were the prison officials. Someone had informed on the whole meeting and on Emam Maleek in particular. The guards were waiting on the yard with their clubs on their sides.

Emam Maleek had no idea that the plan was exposed yet. Before he was about to go to the yard, he performed the late afternoon prayer at ten minutes to six. When he finished, he walked past a guard in the cellblock and the phone rang.

"K-block, Officer Crim speaking."

"Officer Crim, will you send inmate Maleek to the Captain's office," said a case manager on the other line.

"Maleek, hold up. They want you in the Captain's office," yelled out the guard, as Abdul Maleek was moving briskly out the cellblock.

Nodding his head, while saying, "All right," Abdul Maleek knew that something wasn't right. Thinking, something just is not right about this, they must know about the meeting. Abdul Maleek stepped in the Captain's office and saw the case manager first.

"What's going on, Mr. Ross?"

"What's this about you planned a meeting on the yard for all the black groups to attend?"

"I'm on my way to the gym, Mr. Ross. Of course I heard about it like everyone else, but I don't have anything to do with it."

"Well anyway, the Captain wants to see you in his office," the case manager said with some skepticism.

The Captain was a seasoned veteran. He knew all about the prison situation and handled it differently.

"How are you today, Captain Layman?" asked Abdul Maleek.

"I'm doing just fine, Maleek. Have a seat for a moment. Look here, I'm asking you not to go outside at six o'clock, I already know what's going on. My officers have orders to put anyone that goes onto that yard in the hole, and if we don't have the room, we're gong to find some.

Everything is okay now, I got those four bastards locked up now. They won't be coming back out here again. I put them in the cell with the biggest black guys that I could find, I'm asking you to call this thing off, Maleek. Can you do that for me?"

"I don't see any problem with doing that, Captain Ross."

"Do that for me, will you?"

Abdul Maleek headed for the door and into the hallway. He bypassed the exit doors that led to the prison yard, but looked out of one of the windows. The yard had some correction officers on it and the surveillance cameras pointing to the exits.

At the gym was a large group of inmates already waiting. They had been diverted from the yard earlier in the day. Abdul Maleek saw the MB's over by the weight pile.

"As-salaam alaikum, brothers."

"Wa-alaikum salaam."

"I see that everyone was ready, huh, Muntaqim?" the Emam asked to his security chief.

"Yeah, brother, we got word of what happened especially when everybody got turned around when they tried to get on the yard. The guards kept saying that they had the leader in the Captain's office. Right then, I figured that they must have been talking about you."

"I just came from there," said Emam Maleek. "The Captain said that he locked the four bastards up, so I want you to pass the word that the ones who carried out the hit, are locked up."

"You know that these young boys still want some blood."

"I know, but the authorities are on to the whole plan now, plus somebody within the ranks told them my name. That means that we'll have to tighten up, brother, and then when we find that leak, we're going to deal with it."

"I'll be there with you, brother," Abdul Muntaqim said.

CHAPTER 6

LUCASVILLE RIOT AND A FEW CONSEQUENCES

"You do what you gotta do and we'll do what we're gonna do!" The longest, but not the deadliest penitentiary riot took place at the maximum-security prison at Lucasville, Ohio.

There was a claim that there were three groups with different agendas controlling the riot of Lucasville; some Muslim brothers, the Black Gangster Disciples, and the Aryan Brotherhood. The only way that this alliance with the AB was going to work, was that there had to be a cause against the prison and their policies.

The different agendas, such as not being forced to take the tuberculin test, which is a screening tool for tuberculosis, forced integration within the cells and the ease of overcrowding were a few of the many issues brought to the negotiating table, which was televised on national television.

The claim was that a Muslim brother planned and led the riot. He was later given a death penalty indictment in court.

The so-called leader of the Gangster Disciples was used to testify against all the other heads of organizations that were involved in the supposed vote to kill a guard. He got a reduced sentence, the others received a death penalty indictment.

A black correction officer who was a hostage, pretended to have accepted Al-Islam. He did so in the midst of inmates with knives, masks over their faces, blood and some bodies lying around. When he professed that there was no Lord, but Allah, and Muhammad (pbuh) is his Messenger, he was let go.

This same guard then went on national television and got interviewed by the nationally known news personality, Bryant Gumble. In the interview, the guard told Bryant Gumble that he only pretended to accept Al-Islam and that he's not a Muslim.

This was a slap in the face of some Muslims, who felt that he disrespected them. The guard ended up catching a case, which was later dismissed by the judge in his hometown. He was caught driving intoxicated with a loaded gun by his side. His lawyer got him off with this claim; that a Muslim group was going to kill him on the streets, and that the whole Lucasville episode had put so much stress on him that he couldn't cope with the pressure.

Some Consequences after the Riot

Close security prisons within the state of Ohio, took the free weights out, because the weight bars were used to break through some prison walls to get to some guards.

On Easter Day of every year, a heightened sense of security occurs on the part of prison authorities. Certain Muslim communities are watched more closely than others are.

There's an effort on some prison authorities part to make sure that a dominant Muslim leader never rise up again with the power to influence all the other organizations in their midst.

A monetary settlement based off of a lawsuit was won by those inmates who supposedly had nothing to do with the riot. The money is to be split between the inmates and the family of the prison guard who was killed and of course the fees that had to be paid to the lawyers.

GLOSSARY

Chapter 1

Count Time:	The time of day when all prisoners must be accounted for.
Joint:	Prison, Penitentiary
Check in:	When an inmate voluntarily enters an isolated part of the prison for protection.
Strapped:	Always having a knife on ones person.
Boys:	Homosexual, punk, fag.
Zoo-zoo's:	Coffee, chips, candy, cookies.
Bozo:	Reefer, marijuana

Chapter 2

Rolling:	Affiliation
Khutbah:	The sermon given on Friday at Islamic Services.
Bay'at:	Allegiance.
White shirts:	Correction officers with rank; Captains, Lieutenants, and Sergeants.
Shank:	Knives made from fiberglass or steel.

Chapter 4

Sukeenuun:	Knives made from fiberglass or steel.
Amir:	Muslim leader.
Ramadan:	The ninth month of the Islamic calendar.

www.ingramcontent.com/pod-product-compliance
Lightning Source LLC
Chambersburg PA
CBHW030357290526
45785CB00004B/1785